THE BIBLICAL PERIOD FROM ABRAHAM TO EZRA

WILLIAM FOXWELL ALBRIGHT

THE
BIBLICAL PERIOD
FROM
ABRAHAM TO EZRA

HARPER TORCHBOOKS

Harper & Row, Publishers

New York, Hagerstown, San Francisco, London

This book is a revised and expanded version of "The Biblical Period," an essay by Dr. Albright first published in *The Jews: Their History, Culture, and Religion* which was edited by Louis Finkelstein and published by Harper & Brothers in 1949, with revised editions published in 1955 and 1960. The original material is here reprinted by permission.

First HARPER TORCHBOOK edition published 1963 by Harper & Row, Publishers, Inc., New York and Evanston.

80   20 19 18 17 16

CONTENTS

FOREWORD

This little book is a revision and expansion of the first chapter in Louis Finkelstein's two-volume work, *The Jews: Their History, Culture and Religion* (New York, 1949), with a new title. The text was originally written in the summer of 1947, just fifteen years before the date of the present revision. In order to include some treatment of new finds and their significance, as well as a brief account of my own recent work on such figures as Abraham and Samuel, the book is nearly half again as long as the chapter on "The Biblical Period." (The 1950 reprint by the Biblical Colloquium omitted the Bibliography, but added a Chronological Table; we have followed suit, but have revised the Table.)

It must be remembered that this book is only a sketch, and that important figures and episodes in the history of Israel are not even mentioned, in order to make room for others. In particular, we make no attempt to survey the culture, the religious history and the literature of Israel systematically. Readers interested in these aspects of the Old Testament are advised to read John Bright's admirable volume, *A History of Israel* (1959), G. Ernest Wright's *Biblical Archaeology* (1957), my own Penguin paperback, *The Archaeology of Palestine* (latest partial revision, 1960), as well as my books, *From the Stone Age to Christianity* (latest partial revision, 1957) and *Archaeology and the Religion of Israel* (latest partial revision, 1953). My two-volume survey of the history of the religion of Israel was about two-thirds written in 1958-59, and will, I hope, appear within the next few years; progress is this field has been little short of vertiginous, from my point of view.

The foregoing books all reflect my own point of view or that of the group of scholars to which I belong. There are other excellent books which should be read for perspective as well as for content, such as the revised English translation of Martin Noth's *Geschichte Israels* (1950), which has appeared as *The History of Israel*, Yehezkel Kaufmann's *The Religion of Israel* (abridged and translated from the Hebrew by Moshe Greenberg, 1960), Roland de Vaux, *Ancient Israel: Its Life and Institutions* (translated from the original work, *Les institutions de l'Ancien Testament*, 1958-60, by John McHugh, 1961).

It is an unusual pleasure to thank those who have been responsible for the appearance of this little book. My thanks are due particularly to Chancellor Finkelstein, who edited the original contribution and is responsible for its appearance as a Harper Torchbook, to his daughter Emunah, who was my peerless research assistant in 1958-59, to Noel Freedman for his assistance in many ways, to my present research assistant, Herbert Huffmon, whose competence and industry have been invaluable, and to the staff of Harper's who have shown phenomenal patience. Without my wife's unfailing support it would be difficult for me to continue my active scholarly work after formal retirement.

WILLIAM FOXWELL ALBRIGHT

July, 1962

HEBREW BEGINNINGS

I

Hebrew national tradition excels all others in its clear picture of tribal and family origins. In Egypt and Babylonia, in Assyria and Phoenicia, in Greece and Rome, we look in vain for anything comparable. There is nothing like it in the tradition of the Germanic peoples. Neither India nor China can produce anything similar, since their earliest historical memories are literary deposits of distorted dynastic tradition, with no trace of the herdsman or peasant behind the demigod or king with whom their records begin. Neither in the oldest Indic historical writings (the Puranas) nor in the earliest Greek historians is there a hint of the fact that both Indo-Aryans and Hellenes were once nomads who immigrated into their later abodes from the north. The Assyrians, to be sure, remembered vaguely that their earliest rulers, whose names they recalled without any details about their deeds, were tent dwellers, but whence they came had long been forgotten.

In contrast with these other peoples the Israelites preserved an unusually clear picture of simple beginnings, of complex migrations, and of extreme vicissitudes, which plunged them from their favored status under Joseph to bitter oppression after his death. Until recently it was the fashion among biblical historians to treat the patriarchal sagas of Genesis as though they were artificial creations of Israelite scribes of the Divided Monarchy or tales told by imaginative rhapsodists around Israelite campfires during the centuries following their occupation of the country. Eminent names among scholars can be cited for regarding every item of Gen. 11-50 as reflecting late invention, or at least retrojection of events and conditions under the Monarchy into the remote past, about which nothing was thought to have been really known to the writers of later days.

Archaeological discoveries since 1925 have changed all this. Aside from a few die-hards among older scholars, there is scarcely a single biblical historian who has not been impressed by the rapid accumulation of data supporting the substantial historicity of patriarchal tradition. According to the traditions of Genesis the ancestors of Israel were closely related to the semi-nomadic peoples of Trans-Jordan, Syria, the Euphrates basin and North Arabia in the last centuries of the second millennium B.C. and the first centuries of the first millennium. This has been strikingly confirmed by the linguistic data found in recently excavated inscriptions. Genesis derives the ancestors of Israel from Mesopotamia—archaeological evidence agrees. According to Gen. 11:31, Terah, father of Abraham, migrated from Ur-kasdim, that is, from the territory of the great Babylonian city of Ur, to the region of Harran in northwestern Mesopotamia.[1] The British excavations at Ur from 1922 to 1934, illustrated by cuneiform documents from other sites, have proved that Ur was at the height of its prosperity from about 2060 to about 1950 B.C. (low chronology), when it was destroyed by invading Elamites. Ur was partially restored, but during the wars between Samsu-iluna, the Amorite son of the great Hammurapi, and Ilima-Anum in the early seventeenth century it was destroyed and disappears from history for centuries. We may never be able to fix the date of Terah's migration from Ur to Harran, but there can be no doubt that a date about the third quarter of the twentieth century B.C. would suit historical indications remarkably well.

We lack space to outline the evidence which demonstrates beyond reasonable doubt that Hebrew tradition was correct in tracing the Patriarchs directly back to the Balikh Valley in northwestern Mesopotamia. This evidence consists of explicit references to cities like Harran and Nahor (Gen. 24:10), both of which were flourishing in the nineteenth and eighteenth centuries;[2] it consists also of personal, tribal and divine names,[3] and especially of the cosmogonic narratives of Gen. 2-11.[4] The latter are peculiarly significant, because they are closely related to similar material preserved in Assyro-Babylonian tablets, whereas they bear virtually no relation whatever to Canaanite cosmogony as now known from various sources. In

this connection it may be noted that the writer no longer connects the story of Babel with the time of Hammurapi and his
successors (seventeenth-sixteenth centuries B.C.) but rather
with the Babylonian stories relating to the foundation of Babylon by Sargon of Accad, several centuries earlier.[5]

We now know that the age of the Patriarchs, between the
twentieth and sixteenth centuries B.C., was unusually well
adapted for just such movements as those described in the Book
of Genesis. In the twentieth and nineteenth centuries Amorite
chieftains displaced native Accadian (Assyro-Babylonian)
princes in most Mesopotamian districts, and the process was
continued until by the time of the Mari archives in the late
eighteenth century we find Amorites in nearly every important
political post from the Zagros Mountains in western Iran to
the Mediterranean. The term "Amorite," it must be remembered, was originally an Accadian word meaning "westerner";
in the patriarchal age it was applied to all people speaking
Northwest Semitic dialects, including the ancestors of the later
Arameans and Israelites. Among "Amorite" personal names in
these centuries we have a number characteristic also of Hebrew
tradition, such as Abram, Jacob, Laban, Zebulun, Benjamin.[6]
The Mari archives, discovered by a French expedition in 1936,
illustrate the freedom of movement between various parts of
the Amorite world in the late eighteenth century extraordi-
narily well. Trade was widespread and caravans of merchants
were among the commonest sights. The king of Assyria, with
his capital at Assur on the Tigris, negotiated with the prince
of Qatna in central Syria with a view to marrying his son to
the latter's daughter, just as the humbler Abram sent his son
to Nahor near Harran for a similar purpose. To protect traders
and farmers against the still semi-nomadic kinsmen of the
settled Amorites great vigilance was necessary and an elaborate
system of signal fires was devised for rapid communication
over distances.[7]

Numerous recent excavations in sites of this period in Palestine, supplemented by finds made in Egypt and Syria, give us
a remarkably precise idea of patriarchal Palestine, fitting well
into the picture handed down in Genesis. After about 2200
B.C. there was a progressive deterioration of material culture in

the land, accompanied by rapid thinning out of occupation, certainly because of increasing pressure from nomadic and semi-nomadic groups in and around the country. After the nineteenth century nomadic attacks blotted out sedentary occupation all but completely from southern and central Trans-Jordan; it was not until the thirteenth that it became resettled, after some six centuries without appreciable sedentary occupation.[8] Egyptian records of the late twentieth century (published by Kurt Sethe) show that nearly all Palestine and southern Syria were organized along tribal lines, very few towns being mentioned, in strict agreement with the results of excavations. Under Egyptian protection, however, sedentary occupation developed rapidly, until by the late nineteenth century Egyptian records (published by Georges Posener) prove that nearly all western Palestine and southern Syria were organized as city-states, while Trans-Jordan was still in the tribal stage of development.[9] Again archaeology confirms the data provided by written records. In this period, moreover, towns were scattered thinly through the hill country and sedentary occupation was largely restricted to the coastal plains and the broad alluvial valleys of Jezreel and the Jordan. The wanderings of the later Patriarchs are thus correctly limited by tradition to the hill country and the desert Negeb; not a single city of the coastal plains or the broad valleys of the interior is mentioned. (See below for new light on special conditions in the time of Abraham.) Moreover, Egyptian records and excavations at such sites as Gezer and Megiddo in Palestine, Gebal (Byblus), Qatna and Ugarit in Lebanon and Syria prove that Egypt then controlled Palestine, Phoenicia and southern Syria, and that trade between Egypt and Palestine was very active.[10] The famous mural painting of Beni-Hasan, dated about the year 1892 B.C., portrays a visit to Middle Egypt by a little caravan of traveling Semitic smiths and musicians, who provide an excellent background from which to understand Gen. 4:20-22.[11] The picture of movements in the hill country of Palestine, of seasonal migration between the Negeb and central Palestine,[12] and of easy travel to Mesopotamia and Egypt is, accordingly, so perfectly in accord with conditions in the Middle Bronze Age that historical skepticism is quite unwarranted. When we add the fact that our present knowledge of social institutions and customs in another part of northern Mesopotamia in the fifteenth century (Nuzi) has brilliantly illuminated many details in the patriarchal stories which do not fit into the post-Mosaic tradition at all,[13] our case for the substantial historicity of the tradition of the Patriarchs is clinched. This does not, of course, mean that oral tradition, even though based on poetic epics as Cassuto and others have seen, can be treated by the historian as though it were based directly on written records. In many ways the orally transmitted record is superior, but it is peculiarly exposed to the phenomena of refraction and selection of elements suited for epic narrative, regardless of their chronological order.[14] It is, accordingly, uncertain to what extent we can adopt the traditional order of events or the precise motivation attributed to them. Nor can we accept every picturesque detail as it stands in our present narrative. But as a whole the picture in Genesis is historical, and there is no reason to doubt the general accuracy of the biographical details and the sketches of personality which make the Patriarchs come alive with a vividness unknown to a single extrabiblical character in the whole vast literature of the ancient Near East.

In the preceding paragraphs we have described the general archaeological and cultural background of the early Patriarchal Age. During the past fifteen years (1947-1962) it has become possible to pinpoint the background of the stories of Abraham (Gen. 12-24) with a precision wholly undreamed of when the first edition of this survey was written.[15] The meaning of the term 'Apiru- 'Abiru, later 'Ibri, "Hebrew," has now been established; it meant something like "donkey-man, donkey driver, huckster, caravaneer."[16] Originally it may have meant "dusty," with obvious reference to the dust raised by donkeys on a much-travelled road.[17] As we know from a multitude of passages, extending over a millennium, from the late third millennium to the twelfth century B.C., the 'Apiru were as a rule stateless persons of varied ethnic stock, scattered from Elam to Egypt. In the earliest texts, as well as sporadically in documents of even the latest period, they appear as caravaneers, but they were frequently accused or suspected of banditry, and as the donkey caravan trade declined they were forced into other occupations.

The Patriarchal tradition of Israel agrees very well with this picture. Abraham's family is said to have lived at Ur in southern Babylonia ("Ur in the land of the Chaldaeans"),[18] and at Harran and Nahor in northwestern Mesopotamia. Since Ur was the greatest trading city that the world then knew, and since Harran is admirably situated for trade, with a name meaning "Caravan City," the names of these cities alone point to a caravaneering tradition. Furthermore, all the places with which Abraham is connected in Syria and Palestine can be shown to have been important caravan stations; for most of them there is archaeological or documentary evidence of occupation in the nineteenth-eighteenth centuries B.C.[19] In addition to these facts we now know, thanks to the explorations of Nelson Glueck, supplemented by the work of Beno Rothenberg in the Peninsula of Sinai, that there was seasonal occupation along the caravan routes of the Negeb of Israel and northern Sinai during the same centuries. Even more remarkable is the fact that in most of the areas where sites of this period are found, little or nothing from earlier or later periods occurs. This is especially true of the caravan routes between the Negeb and Egypt. Gen. 20:1 may best be rendered: "And Abraham departed from there to the Negeb, keeping between Kadesh and the Wall (of Egypt), while he was a resident alien at Gerar." In other words, his house and family were at Gerar on the edge of the desert Negeb while he spent his time in northern Sinai leading caravans. It is no accident that the great site of Gerar, discovered recently by Israelis at Tell Abu Hureirah, is also shown by archaeological remains to have been occupied in the nineteenth and eighteenth centuries B.C.[20]

We know from Old-Assyrian documents found in Cappadocia and from Egyptian inscriptions set up at Serabit el-Khadim in western Sinai that the nineteenth century B.C. was perhaps the high point of donkey caravan trade in antiquity. There are a great many references to donkeys, whose number is listed in contemporary Egyptian texts as ranging from 200 to 600 for each caravan.[21] A special breed of black donkeys was favored in the north, whereas light-colored donkeys were preferred in Egypt and Sinai. Camels were, of

course, known, and there may have been some sporadic do-
mestication, but there is no evidence for camel caravans or
raiding expeditions before the twelfth century B.C. Presumably
camels were gradually domesticated in eastern Arabia during
the middle centuries of the second millennium.[22]

That Abraham (Abram) was an important figure in his day
seems probable, since the traditions about him appear to have
been handed down orally for many centuries with little
change. The narrative in Gen. 14, describing Abraham's triumph over the four kings of the East, has long been recognized
as containing very archaic features.[23] An underlying poem
going back to the Bronze Age has been surmised. The names
themselves can also be closely paralleled among personal and
tribal names from the early second millennium B.C., and several words occurring only here in the Hebrew Bible can be
identified with similar words in the inscriptions of the period.
References to places in Trans-Jordan and the Negeb of western Palestine fit in extremely well with the nineteenth century
B.C., to which we may provisionally attribute the historical
nucleus of the chapter. If it was handed down for centuries by
word of mouth, we can illustrate the mode of transmission by
quoting the Song of Deborah, which presumably used much
older material (since donkey caravans, though mentioned in
the Amarna Tablets, must have been losing ground rapidly by
the twelfth century B.C.) :

> In the days of Shamgar ben Anath
>   . . . the caravans ceased,
> And those who traveled the caravan roads
>   followed winding paths.
> . . . .
> O riders on tawny she-asses,
>   O ye who walk on the roads, attend!
> At the sound of the cymbals,
>   between the watering places (?) ,
> There they will chant the triumphs of Yahweh,
>   the triumphs of his warriors (?) in Israel.

Gen. 15 also contains some exceedingly important reminiscences from the early Patriarchal Age. For example, it has
become clear that the enigmatic passage in 15:2-4, referring to

an Eliezer who is nowhere else mentioned, means simply that Abraham's legal heir (*ben beto*) was Eliezer of Damascus, but that Abraham wanted to have a son who would become his legal heir.[24] In fifteenth-century Nuzi, from which we have so many early cuneiform parallels to Patriarchal customary law, a man who was in debt or who needed supplies would often adopt a wealthy money-lender as his heir. The basic reason for this legal fiction was obviously that in the customary law of that region a man was not supposed to alienate ancestral property. When there was no other recourse, a man might adopt a money-lender, who would then inherit his property. Since Damascus was one of the most important caravan centers of that age, the situation is obvious; a caravan leader would have to purchase donkeys and other supplies, whose acquisition would be impossible unless he could establish credit. In a somewhat similar way Hillel the Elder is said to have instituted the *prozbul*, by which it became possible for a debt to be repaid after the next sabbatical year by the device of turning the collection over to the court; a Jew might borrow money before a sabbatical year by declaring before the court that he would pay it back through the court. This made it practicable for the lender to continue operations without fearing the approach of the seventh year, while the would-be borrower could more easily find a man willing to lend him money.

The account of the covenant between Yahweh and Abraham in the same chapter is replete with archaisms; its antiquity has been established by E. A. Speiser. Here we have an example of the central place held in early Hebrew religion by the special god of a man with whom he made a solemn compact, according to the terms of which the god would protect him and his family in return for an oath of allegiance. This is a primitive form of the suzerainty treaty which we shall discuss below. In the Late Bronze Age the word *beritu*, Hebrew *berit*, "compact," appears in Syria and Egypt (where it was a Semitic loanword) in connection with contract labor and contractual hiring of persons listed in a given document.[25] It is only natural that the contract relationship should be transferred to religion by the early Hebrews, since their caravaneering and trading activities must have led to innumerable contracts and treaties with heads of states and tribes, local dignitaries, merchants, caravaneers, etc. The emphasis on a personal or family god, as distinct from a deity worshiped in a given temple, also points to the wandering life of the early Hebrew caravaneers. It is noteworthy that the closest parallels in the Patriarchal Age come from the Assyrian merchant colonies of the nineteenth century B.C. in Cappadocia, and that nearly all of Albrecht Alt's parallels come from Nabataean or Palmyrene, as well as later Syrian inscriptions belonging to trading or caravaneering families.

In the same archaic chapter we have definite traditional evidence about the length of time believed to have elapsed between the beginning of the Egyptian sojourn which followed the Patriarchal Age proper, and the return to Palestine. Gen. 15:13-16 has been generally misunderstood; the word *dor* did not mean "generation" in early Hebrew, but "lifetime," like Etruscan-Roman *saeculum;* the Arabic cognate *dahrun* often means "lifetime" (originally "cycle"), Syriac *dara* is defined as "80 years," and the word *darum* appears in an inscription of Shamshi-Adad I of Assyria also in the meaning "lifetime" (seven *daru* elapsed between the climax of the empire of Accad and his own reign, i.e., between *c.* 2250 and *c.* 1750 B.C.). In verse 13 the equivalent of four lifetimes is explicitly given as "400 years." If we allow three lifetimes for the periods represented by Abraham, Isaac and Jacob, it would seem that early Hebrew tradition allowed seven lifetimes or roughly seven centuries for the entire period from Abraham to the Conquest of Canaan. That there were gaps in the genealogies is to be expected, since most oral tradition tends to skip over obscure or uninteresting periods. Recent studies by anthropologists and archaeologists have shown that there were gaps in the genealogical tradition of such regions as the Sudan, Rhodesia, Polynesia and Arabia.[26] There is thus not the slightest real basis for recent attempts to reduce the date of Abraham to the Late Bronze Age, in the fifteenth or even fourteenth century B.C. Quite aside from arguments of the type illustrated above, we now have a great deal of evidence from personal and place names, almost all of which is against such unwarranted telescoping of traditional data.

II
THE AGE OF MOSES

There has been a persistent effort by many scholars to dis-
credit the Israelite tradition of a prolonged sojourn in Egypt
before the time of Moses. It is true that these narratives, as we
have them, were modernized about the tenth century B.C., the
personal and geographical names of older tradition being in
part revised to suit contemporary Egyptian nomenclature.
Since almost exactly the same thing was done some seven centuries later by the Greek translators of Genesis (or by their
Hebrew scribal source), the mere fact of such revision does not
disprove the authenticity of the underlying tradition.[27] We
now know from a mass of corroborative evidence to what a
profound extent the northern part of Egypt, especially the
northeastern Delta, became semitized during the period in
question.[28] Semitic influences poured into Egypt during the
Twelfth Dynasty, when (as noted above) Palestine, Phoenicia
and southern Syria belonged to the sphere of Egyptian suzerainty. In the eighteenth century these influences increased
rapidly in significance, and before the end of this century
Semites had made themselves masters of much of Egypt.[29] The
Hyksos conquerors are now known to have been mainly—perhaps entirely—of Northwest Semitic stock, closely akin to the
Hebrews, who probably formed one of their component elements.[30] Biblical Hebrew names like Jacob and Hur figure
among the lists of their chieftains and nobles; in fact, the early
Hyksos "Pharaoh" represented by the most scarabs was called
"Jacob" (*Ya'qub*, the short form of his full name *Ya'qub-
har*). There are numerous details in Hebrew tradition which
square so completely with Egyptian data that an intimate connection between the Hebrew settlement in Egypt and the
Hyksos conquest may be considered certain. We cannot say

more with confidence because of the almost complete lack of Egyptian historical inscriptions during the whole Hyksos age. If this gap in our knowledge is ever filled, we shall probably owe it to some unexpected find of cuneiform tablets in Syria or Palestine.

The Hyksos were finally crushed by the founder of the Eighteenth Dynasty, Amosis I (c. 1570-1545), who stormed Tanis (Zoan) and destroyed the last Semitic garrisons in Egypt about 1550 B.C. There is no reason to think that the Semites were driven out of the country, though some of the leaders and the more nomadic elements may have retreated to Palestine. Judging from contemporary documents, those who escaped slaughter were enslaved or were permitted to remain in the region around Tanis as serfs. There is, accordingly, every reason to regard Amosis as the "Pharaoh who knew not Joseph" of Ex. 1:8. In tradition, however, there is always a strong tendency to pass silently over periods when there is nothing exciting to report. Hence Hebrew tradition slipped without realizing the shift from Amosis to Sethos I, who began to rebuild the long-neglected city of Tanis, after his accession to the throne of the Nineteenth Dynasty about 1309 B.C. In the interim Semitic influence became increasingly powerful in Egypt. It may now be considered as certain that the term 'Apiru, where used in Egyptian inscriptions of the fifteenth-twelfth centuries B.C., had the same basic meaning as "Hebrew" in early times—i.e., "caravaneer."[31] It is quite possible that the word meant just that in Egyptian usage and that it never received the ethnic connotations which it certainly had in Palestine toward the end of the second millennium. In the early fifteenth century the 'Apiru appear as vintagers in the northeastern Delta, which was the chief vine-growing area in Egypt at that time. Since vintagers from this district mentioned in labels or dockets from the reigns of Amenophis III (early fourteenth century) and Rameses II (thirteenth century), bear Semitic names or names designating them as Asiatics, it is hard to separate them from the Hebrews, who were settled in the same region according to biblical tradition. How easy it was for caravaneers to resort to vine-growing and wine-making as a supplement to, or substitute for their normal

occupation may be inferred also from a remarkable passage in
the Blessing of Judah (Gen. 49:11) :

> He tethered his donkey to a vine,
>   to a grapevine his young donkey,
> While he washed out his garment with wine,
>   his robe with the blood of grapes.

Though the Blessing of Jacob as a whole does not antedate
the late eleventh century B.C., this passage is much earlier, as
illustrated by the fact that the three words which discribe a
young donkey in the first bicolon are identical with the three
words used to define the kind of donkey sacrificed by the tribes
of northern Mesopotamia, while solemnizing a treaty, according to the Mari texts. The words are not only identical but
they appear in the same order. Another striking archaism is
"the blood of grapes," corresponding to Ugaritic "blood of
trees" used in parallelism with the same word for "wine."

The worship of Canaanite gods introduced by the Hyksos,
such as Baal, Horon, Resheph, and of goddesses like Ashtaroth
(Astarte), Anath and Asherah (called "Holiness," Heb.
Qodesh) increased more or less steadily until it reached a
climax in the time of Moses (thirteenth century B.C.).[32]

Direct information about the language and religion of the
Egyptianized Semites of northern Egypt also comes from the
Proto-Sinaitic inscriptions of Serabit el-Khadim in western
Sinai. Here Flinders Petrie discovered a number of archaic
alphabetic inscriptions in 1905; they were partly deciphered by
Alan Gardiner in 1915. Many more inscriptions were added to
the list, and in 1948[33] the writer succeeded in advancing the
decipherment materially, at the same time that he brought
new proof for the correctness of Petrie's date about 1500. In
1957 the writer continued the decipherment of 1948, with
satisfactory results; the corrected decipherment was confirmed
in essential respects by a little prism, discovered at Lachish and
published by Olga Tufnell in 1958.[34] The prism corroborates
both the basic interpretation and the dating, since the forms of
letters are virtually identical and the prism is dated in the
reign of Amenophis II (c. 1436-1420).

The authors of the inscriptions wrote in a Northwest-

Semitic dialect which was substantially identical with South Canaanite, but had some interesting similarities to Ugaritic; there is little which would not fit well into Proto-Hebrew, as reconstructed for pre-Mosaic times. They had been living in Egypt so long that their divinities were partly Egyptianized. For instance, the god El was identified with the great creator god, Ptah of Memphis; the goddess Baalath, "The Lady," was identified with Hathor. Less well known are the deities "He of the Wine Press," presumably referring to the Egyptian god Shesmu, worshiped particularly in Memphis and the eastern Delta; Shesmu was specifically god of the wine press, since his name was written with the hieroglyph for "wine press" and he is said as early as the twenty-fourth century B.C. to bring wine for the deceased king. By the fourteenth century B.C. the Semites were identifying the "Lord of the Wine Press" with their own El, as we know from the Lachish prism, which labels a characteristic representation of Ptah as *Dhu-gitti* (*Dhu-ginti* in the somewhat earlier Proto-Sinaitic inscriptions). We seem also to find the Egyptian gods Osiris and Anubis referred to as "He Who is Over the Meadow" and "He of the Jackals." The goddess "She of the Serpents" is presumably Asherah who, as Qudshu, "Holiness," brandished serpents in her outstretched hands. Qudshu had already become one of the popular goddesses of Egypt. Since six of our thirty or so inscriptions are found on objects of Egyptian origin or accompanying Egyptian representations, it would be very strange if there were not some Egyptian influence on the pantheon of the inscriptions. Specifically Hebrew deities also were worshiped, to judge from a personal name borne by a petty official of the late fourteenth century, "Sadde-'ammi," that is, "Shadde-'ammi" in later Hebrew pronunciation.[35]

The god Shaddai, properly "The One of the Mountains, Mountain-god,"[36] attributed in Israelite tradition to the Patriarchs, was certainly a principal deity of Israel in the days of Moses, as we know from the fact that the name is a component of three personal names borne by Israelites living in the time of Moses. Since one of these names is identical (in reverse order of elements) with this Sadde-'ammi, it is quite likely that it belongs to a Hebrew who was an older contemporary of Moses. Some two generations earlier there had flourished another high Egyptian official with a Semitic name who may have been Hebrew by race, Yanhamu, Egyptian commissioner in Palestine.

By 1300 B.C. the stage was set, culturally and religiously, for the emergence of a heroic figure like Moses. He himself bore an Egyptian name only slightly altered in the speech of later Israel, and Egyptian names such as Phinehas, Hophni and Merari were common among his relatives.[37] At that time, after intimate political and cultural contact between Egypt and Palestine for some seven centuries, there were thousands—perhaps scores of thousands—of Semites living as slaves, serfs, merchants and nobles in Egypt, with thousands of Egyptians in Palestine and Phoenicia. We have already referred to the Canaanite gods adopted into the Egyptian pantheon; hundreds of Semitic words (Canaanite and Hebrew) occur in the native Egyptian literature of the period, especially in the thirteenth century, in which no literary composition failed to be sprinkled with them. Bilingualism must have been characteristic of the Ramesside capital at Tanis, around which lay the land of Goshen. In contemporary Palestine we find no fewer than four scripts used side by side to write Canaanite, and learned scribes wrote Accadian, the medium of international communication employed at that time in the entire ancient Near East. It would, accordingly, be passing strange if Moses were not at home in both Egyptian and Canaanite, as well as in his native Hebrew (which was only a dialectal variant of Canaanite). Moreover, the entire cosmopolitan world of the day must have been familiar to his eyes and ears in and around the Egyptian capital at Tanis. The reconstruction of Tanis begun by Sethos I was continued by his son, the Pharaoh of the Exodus, Rameses II, who called it "House of Rameses" (Raamses, Ex. 1:11; cf. Gen. 47:11, where "the land of Rameses" is the same district as the "plain of Tanis" in Psalm 78:12, 43).[38] Since it was the capital of Egypt and was also situated on the Egyptian frontier toward Syria, an Egyptian scribe was justified in speaking of it as the "front of every foreign country, the end of Egypt." He goes on to describe the beauty of its gorgeous buildings and the importance of its military role as the base of operations in foreign lands, where chariot horses were inspected, foot soldiers were marshaled, and warships were moored. Another scribe waxes dithyrambic in picturing the wealth and resources of the city and its environs, emphasizing also the fact that it was an important seaport. In a stele found at Beth-shan in Palestine, dated in 1281 B.C., it is said that "He [Rameses II] puts the Asiatics to flight, pacifying the war that had flared up everywhere; those who wish come to him together in humility at his fortress of life and prosperity, House of Rameses, Great of Victories."[39]

The religion of Egypt in the fourteenth and thirteenth centuries B.C. is better known than at any other period, thanks to the great wealth of inscriptions and monumental representations which have come down to us. At the beginning of the fourteenth century Egypt was dominated by the priesthood of the god Amun at Thebes, whose synthetic figure had gradually absorbed the most important deities, such as Re of Heliopolis (Heb. On, home of Joseph's wife), and had become far more important than that of any other Egyptian deity. In fact, just at this time we find Amun-Re exalted in hymns as the father of all other gods, the maker of heaven and earth, creator of mankind. About 1365 B.C. the young Amenophis IV (c. 1370-1353), apparently influenced by his extraordinary mother, Teye, followed an unidentified adviser in breaking completely with the cult of Amun, which was replaced by a solar monotheism centering about the solar disk, Aten. For over fifteen years this monotheistic heresy held sway over Egypt, the old polytheism being repressed with such violence that later Egypt remembered the young king only as "the criminal of Akhetaten" (name of his capital at Tell el-Amarna). Though some writers have gone much too far in connecting the monotheism of Moses with the cult of the Aten, it is probable that there is some indirect connection.[40] In the first place, the people of northern Egypt were restive under the ecclesiastical tyranny of the priests af Amun and did not take kindly to its restoration after Akhenaten's death. In the second place, we have now some long hymns from the thirteenth century which show that the religion of Amun itself had been considerably modified in the preceding two centuries in the direction of syncretism and universalism, with frequent reminiscence of the style and wording of the hymns to the Aten found in a number of the tombs of Amarna.[41]

Among the clearest illustrations of ideas common to Atenism and Mosaism are the exclusive monotheism of both (like the God of Israel in Ex. 20:3, Aten is the god "beside whom there is none other"), the emphasis on the "Teaching" ("Torah" in Israel), and the constant stress on the one God as creator of everything (Aten, like Yahweh, is the god "who creates what comes into existence"). On the other hand, there were many fundamental differences, especially in ethics, between the Aten heresy of Egypt and Mosaic monotheism. Thanks to these far-reaching differences the religion of Moses was incomparably more qualified to move mankind than was the selfish sentimentalism of Amarna.

The Ramesside society in which Moses grew to manhood two generations after the collapse of the Aten heresy was probably the most cosmopolitan hitherto known to the ancient world, as we have shown above. Its religion was equally composite. In the capital itself the great Canaanite gods Baal and Horon, with the goddesses Anath and Astarte, were worshiped on a par with the native Egyptian deities Seth and Horus, Nephthys and Isis, with which they were identified. Egyptian adaptations of several Canaanite myths have been discovered. Egyptian magical compositions of this period are full of Semitic charms and myths. The picture in contemporary Canaan was similar, with Egyptian temples and cults springing up all over the country, the divine craftsman Ptah of Memphis being identified with Koshar, Hathor with Baalath of Byblus, and so on.

Yet the religious picture of Moses's youth was, by and large, singularly repulsive. Among the Canaanites practices considered shockingly immoral by pious Israelites were inextricably bound up with religion. Ritual prostitution of both sexes was rampant, and the variety of evil practices is attested by the multiplicity of names employed to designate these "professions." The *cinaedus* (homosexual) formed a recognized guild in Canaanite temples, and there were other groups which combined dancing and singing with divination in a peculiarly unholy union. Snake worship and human sacrifice were rife. The "Creatress of the Gods" (Asherah) was represented as a beautiful naked prostitute, called "Holiness" in both Canaan and Egypt. The two other principal Canaanite goddesses, Anath and Astarte (Heb. Ashtaroth), are called "the great goddesses which conceive but do not bear," and the rape of Anath by Baal formed a standing theme in Canaanite mythology, in spite of the fact that she was at the same time regularly called "the Virgin." Anath is represented as a naked woman astride a stallion, brandishing her lance; in Canaanite literature she figures in scenes of incredible ferocity.[42]

Among the Egyptians religion stood on a considerably higher plane, but was still anything but an edifying spectacle much of the time. The worship of animals, relatively unimportant in contemporary Canaan, was characteristic of almost every part of Egypt. Egyptian myths swarmed with crudities; for instance, creation was generally described as an act of sexual self-abuse on the part of the divine creator. Moreover, the relation between religion and ethics in Egypt had deteriorated considerably since the early second millennium, as a result of the rapid spread and concomitant degradation of funerary beliefs and practices. Not long before the fifteenth century B.C. an elaborate mortuary ritual, restricted to kings in the Old Empire and extended to include nobles in the Middle Empire, had been further extended to cover anyone who possessed the necessary pecuniary means. In the Book of the Dead and related works we possess the funerary ritual of the Mosaic Age. In spite of the comparatively high ethical standards of the Negative Confession[43] and the judgment before Osiris, it became possible for anyone to assure himself a happy existence in the hereafter by suitable expenditure of his substance for proper burial and for preparation of all necessary magical spells and instructions to accompany him in the journey after death. Since an astonishingly high proportion of the per capita wealth of the country was devoted to the construction of tombs and their subsequent endowment, as well as to the funerals themselves, with the costly embalming of corpses and expensive processions and entertainments that characterized them, it is easy to understand what an abuse this entire phase of Egyptian religion had become by the time of Moses. Small wonder that the new faith reacted violently against all kinds of sacred prostitution and human sacrifice, against magic and divination, and against funerary rites and cult of the dead!

As against the decadence of contemporary Egyptian and Canaanite religion, Moses drew inspiration from the simple traditions of his own Hebrew people and the stern sexual code of the nomads, among whom he spent much of his early manhood before the Exodus. Rejecting all mythology (in accordance with the example of Amarna and doubtless of other abortive efforts to reform religion for which we have no direct information), Moses kept a few traditional appellations of deity, which he now identified with the new figure of Yahweh, which may possibly be older than he but cannot have had any prior importance. Among these names, which we know from the earliest religious poetry of Israel, such as the Oracles of Balaam,[44] were *El* ("The Powerful One"), *Elyon* or *Eli* ("The Exalted One," used by the Canaanites as an appellation of Baal, the great storm-god, king of the gods),[45] *Zur* ("The Mountain") and *Shaddai* (see above). Just as the Canaanites had sometimes used the plural of *el*, "god," to indicate "totality of the gods" (as, for instance, in the Canaanite Amarna letters) so the Israelites used *Elohim* to stress the unity and universality of God.

In the Torah we have, carefully collected and arranged, a considerable body of civil and cultic legislation. These laws and regulations are couched in different wording, showing complex sources. They have been preserved for us in documents of different ages—all relatively early. Yet there is a basic similarity about their cultural and religious background which makes it impossible not to attribute their origin to the beginnings of organized Israelite monotheism—in other words, to Moses. The cultic laws never mention the Temple, while the civil laws reflect a period before the institution of the Monarchy and the appointment of magistrates by the king. Moreover, in recent decades it has become certain that the Book of the Covenant in Ex. 21-23 is part of a once much longer Hebrew analogue to the Codes of Ur-Nammu, Lipit-Ishtar, Eshnunna and Hammurapi, the Assyrian and Hittite legal

codes, and similar legislation, all belonging to the period between 2100 and 1100 B.C.[46] The Book of the Covenant reflects an agricultural society of patriarchal type and simple
mores; it is very different in these respects from both Babylonian and Hittite aristocratic feudalism, in which payments
of money replace corporal punishment, especially where su-
periors are convicted of crimes against inferiors. It is at the
same time, however, much more humane than the draconic
Middle Assyrian laws, which reflect a singularly harsh attempt
to maintain traditional mores in a highly organized urban
civilization. It is, in any case, incredible that the Book of the
Covenant should reflect Canaanite jurisprudence in either
spirit or details, though we may freely concede some Canaanite
influence on formulation and legal terminology, much of it
ultimately Mesopotamian in origin. The standard framework
of the Hebrew case laws is "when . . . provided that . . .
then," as in all known early Babylonian, Assyrian and Hittite
laws.

If we turn to the Priestly Code, a similar situation develops;
in it we have substantially the sacrificial and ritual practice
of the Tabernacle as transmitted by tradition from the period
before Solomon's Temple, just as in corresponding sections of
the Mishna we possess a traditional account of the practice
of Herod's Temple. How much of this ritual goes back to
Moses himself would be idle to conjecture in the present state
of our knowledge; the spirit and much of the detail may be
considered as antedating the Conquest of Canaan—in other
words, as going back to Mosaic origins.

To Albrecht Alt we owe recognition of an extremely important fact: that there is an element in both civil and cultic
legislation of the Torah which was specifically Israelite and
which went back to the beginnings of Israel—in other words,
it was specifically Mosaic.[47] This element is the apodictic legislation which we know best from the Ten Commandments,
consisting of short injunctions, mostly couched in imperative
form: "Thou shalt (not)!" The apodictic laws of the Torah
reflect a monotheistic system with very lofty ethical standards.
It is not necessary to insist that all this legislation goes back
to the Mosaic period in its present form; it was long trans-

mitted orally, and wording must have been modified in the course of the centuries, while relatively primitive injunctions were replaced by others which were better suited to a more advanced society.

The figure of Moses completely dominates the tradition of the Exodus and the Wanderings. It is, accordingly, impossible to picture the movements in question as though they were normal displacements of nomadic tribes. On the contrary, it took both Moses's unusual qualities of leadership and a sequence of extraordinary events, vividly portrayed for us by tradition, to induce his followers to flee from their Egyptian oppressors into the desert. After many generations in the northeastern Delta the Hebrew peasants and shepherds had become accustomed to the odious corvée and to endure the treatment by which Sethos I and his son evidently hoped to reduce the preponderance of Semites in the region around their new capital without losing the advantage of a rich source of slave labor for the state; the alternative of risking all in a desperate break for freedom and even more perilous trek through the wild desert of the Sinai Peninsula did not appeal to them. Fortunately Moses prevailed, and his mob of serfs and slaves of every possible origin (Heb. *asafsuf* and *erebrab*) became crystallized around the tribal nucleus of Israel into a new people, with a new faith and an unparalleled mission in world history.

Having successfully negotiated the difficult barriers imposed by the great Papyrus Marsh (*yam suf*) and the Egyptian frontier posts and punitive measures, the mob of Moses's followers escaped into the desert. Though we have a number of very old traditions regarding details of their generation ("forty years") in the desert and in Trans-Jordan, it is quite impossible to reconstruct the exact sequence of events. Some things are, however, clear. Moses had great difficulty in organizing and disciplining his followers, and there were many serious setbacks, among which we hear of an abortive invasion of the extreme southern fringe of Canaan from the Israelite base at Kadesh-barnea. Since the territory south of Canaan was occupied by nomadic Amalekites, while the fertile regions of Seir and Moab were held by tribes traditionally related to Israel, which were then in the process of settling down,[48] the

Israelites were seriously handicapped for want of room. Moreover, they were compelled by their flocks of sheep and goats, with the accompanying donkeys, to remain close to sources of water, like the oasis of Kadesh. Hence, after it had become evident that Israel was too weak to break through the belt of strongly fortified mounds at the extreme south of Canaan, it was decided to move past Edom and Moab into Trans-Jordan, where the situation was far more favorable. And so it was: the land of the Amorites, which included later Gilead and Ammon, had not been settled long at that time, and towns were sprinkled but thinly over an extensive territory. Moreover, west of this thin zone of fortresses were the forested hills of Gilead, designed by nature for agricultural settlement, but still almost entirely virgin. It was here that the Israelites were able to win their first victories and to establish themselves solidly before invading Canaan.[49] It was here that Moses died at the height of his powers (Deut. 34:7) : "His eye was not dim nor his natural force abated!"

While we do not have material for a satisfactory biography of Moses, nor data for a narrative history of the Exodus, we do have much more evidence than is commonly supposed. The oldest information is generally preserved in verse form or in prose whose poetic origin is transparent. Thanks to the Ugaritic epics and shorter religious hymns (mostly composed in oral form about the first half of the second millennium B.C. in Phoenicia and its hinterland) we can now place the poetic literature of early Israel in its historical setting. By careful arrangement of stylistic forms according to internal evidence from otherwise datable literature, we can say that the Song of Miriam in Ex. 15 is the earliest preserved Hebrew poem of any length, and that the Song of Deborah (middle or late twelfth century B.C.) is definitely later from a purely stylistic point of view. The Oracles of Balaam apparently belong between them, but in part reflect a different stylistic tradition. Numerous verse quotations and reminiscences strewn through Exodus and Numbers show the high antiquity of the tradition underlying the prose narratives in which they are embedded. We can, therefore, be sure of the essential historicity of the Mosaic tradition solely on the ground of its very old poetic content. Curiously enough, entire schools of modern scholarship are still convinced that scarcely any biblical poetic composition can be as early as the oldest prose (excepting the Song of Deborah and a few short poems and scraps, chiefly in Numbers). This view flies directly in the face of the well-known fact that outside of Israel all datable literary prose of the Old World is later than the earliest verse in the language to which the prose and verse belong. As we have just seen, the evidence of style agrees with historical analogy, placing the burden of proof squarely on the shoulders of literary critics, who tend almost invariably to date biblical poetry as late as possible.

For instance, a standard introduction to the Old Testament published twenty years ago,[50] dates the Song of Miriam (Ex. 15:1-18) in the late fifth century B.C., though admitting that 15:21 (actually only a doublet of 15:1, serving as title of the triumphal song)[51] may go back to early times. As we have seen, this composition is closer in style (as well as in vocabulary and grammar) to pre-Mosaic poetry than anything comparable in the Bible. According to this introduction the author of the poem even refers in 15:17 to "the Second Temple, completed in 516." This verse runs:

> Thou wilt bring it and wilt plant it (the people)
> In the mount of thine inheritance.

Similarly in the Baal Epic of Ugarit, Baal refers to Mount Zaphon as "the mount of mine inheritance"; Zaphon is explicitly identified in the Ugaritic texts with Mount Casius, the Canaanite sacred mountain.[52] The word for "inheritance" is the same, and this and the following verse contain several other close resemblances between Ugaritic and Hebrew poetic passages and expressions. It is not only improbable, it is absurd to date the Song of Miriam eight centuries too late on the strength of evidence which actually points in the opposite direction.

If we turn from poetry to prose tradition, we may mention one of many illustrations of its antiquity, pointed out by the writer in 1954. The authenticity of the names of the midwives in Ex. 1:15, Shiphrah and Puah, has often been denied by modern scholars, but both names have turned up as names of women among the Northwestern Semites of the second millennium B.C., one attested in the eighteenth century, the other in the fourteenth.[53] A detail such as this is in a sense trivial, but both names are authentic early names and together they indicate that the story of the midwives is very ancient.

III

THE CONQUEST OF PALESTINE

Thanks to an enormous increase in the materials at our disposal since 1930, our picture of Canaanite history and civilization at the time of the Hebrew Conquest has become far clearer than it was. To the domain of Canaanite culture then belonged the entire coastland of Palestine and Syria from the Egyptian frontier south of Gaza to the northern boundary of Ugarit, on the coast southwest of Antioch. Eastward the borders were fluctuating, and there is much confusion in tradition between Canaanites and Amorites, whose language and culture differed so little that it is hard to find a satisfactory criterion for use of these names. Originally the term "Canaan" was applied almost certainly to Phoenicia proper as the land of purple dye, whereas "Amorite" was a general term used in Mesopotamia to designate all Northwestern Semites as "Westerners." Later "Canaan" was extended southward and eastward, while "Amor" (Amurru) was adopted in the West as a designation for a large parent state in eastern Syria, to which smaller states later traced their origin. "Canaanite" higher culture, both religious and literary, went back to age-old tradition along the eastern shore of the Mediterranean, whereas "Amorite" higher culture was strongly influenced by Sumero-Accadian civilization.

At the time of the Israelite Conquest, western Palestine had been for many centuries subject to Egyptian rule. Ever since about 2000 B.C. it had been nominally dependent on Egypt, but in the eighteenth century the Egyptian crown became too weak to exercise any real authority in the country. Toward the end of the century Northwest Semitic tribes occupied northern Egypt, and an ephemeral Semitic empire was established with its center at Avaris, later called Tanis (Heb. Zoan).[54] After

Amosis's expulsion of the Hyksos (c. 1550 B.C.) the native Egyptian pharaohs fell heir to the Hyksos heritage in Palestine and Syria. Rebellions were frequent but invariably abortive. Under the heavy hand of Egyptian bureaucrats and garrisons of slave troops, the country suffered, as may be seen from the relatively continuous decline in the arts which has been demonstrated by archaeological explorations in the past thirty-five years.[55] The exorbitant demands of the crown were greatly swelled by the attempts of Egyptian officials of all grades to enrich themselves during their periods in office. Moreover, owing both to inefficient administration and to dishonesty, supplies for the Nubian and other slave troops which maintained order in the provinces were often held up, and the unfortunate troops had to resort to pillage and banditry in order to live. Both Egyptian and cuneiform documents of the age contain many vivid illustrations of the situation.

At the same time that the wealth of the country and the morale of its inhabitants were slowly drained away by a rapacious foreign government, the native Canaanite princes, who were allowed to continue in their places under the watchful eyes of Egyptian commissioners, were progressively weakened in power and increased in number. Between the time of the Amarna Tablets (c. 1380-1350 B.C.) and the principal phase of the Israelite conquest under Joshua, the number of autonomous princes (sometimes called "kings" in the Amarna Tablets, just as in the Book of Joshua) in southern Palestine appears to have doubled. Excavations have shown (e.g., at Debir, Eglon) that some of the Canaanite "royal cities" of Joshua's time played an entirely different role in the Amarna Age. At the same time there seems to have been a tendency to scatter out from the larger centers and to settle in smaller places, owing partly perhaps to the desire to escape direct control by Egyptian officials and native princes and partly to the fact that cisterns were beginning to come into use, making it possible to establish settlements in places far from a direct source of water (stream or fountain).

The Canaanite population had a sharp class division between the hereditary nobility, largely non-Semitic, and the dependent *khupshu* class, which was only half free, being bound to the soil but possessing certain personal and property rights.[56] There was also a considerable number of trained craftsmen, whose skill and industry made their towns known abroad; but we do not know what their social status was. In addition there was a large slave population. Characteristic of the Amarna Age in all parts of Canaan was a semi-nomadic class called 'Apiru in the Amarna and other cuneiform tablets from Palestine and Syria, as well as in the Egyptian inscriptions. These people are a class rather than an ethnic group, though occasionally the term appears to be used of a specific people rather than a class. As already pointed out,[57] the 'Apiru were originally donkey drivers, hucksters and caravaneers, but after the decline of donkey caravaneering in the eighteenth and seventeenth centuries B.C. they took up other activities to supplement the dwindling donkey caravan trade. Meanwhile their numbers seem to have increased greatly, and they frequently appear as bandits or condottieri. At one time the chief of the 'Apiru was powerful enough to be the target of a coalition between the prince of Jerusalem and his southern allies, on the one hand, and the princes of Accho and Achshaph in the Plain of Acre, on the other. This chieftain was presumably Lab'ayu, who later controlled almost the entire hill country of central Palestine. Shechem may have been his capital; at all events it is mentioned as a town which had come under 'Apiru control. After his death, his sons kept the surrounding Palestinian chieftains in a state of constant uproar. As we shall see at the end of this chapter, these 'Apiru cannot be separated from the biblical Hebrews who lived in Palestine in pre-Mosaic times.

After our earlier sketch it is not necessary to go into detail here about the religion of the Canaanites; suffice it to repeat that their religious beliefs and practices were both crude and depraved by Israelite standards. It is not, however, true that their religion was primitive in the sense of lacking organized priesthood, temple service and pantheon. Quite the contrary! Thanks to the results of the excavations of M. Schaeffer at Ugarit since 1929, supplemented and confirmed by other work elsewhere, we now know that the Canaanites had a great many temples and shrines, adorned with idols, that they had elaborate

priestly institutions, and that their pantheon was no whit less
highly organized than the pantheons of Egypt, Babylonia, the
Hittites, or the nearly contemporary Homeric Greeks. At the
head of their pantheon were the figures of El, slightly remote
from the human scene, and Baal, the great storm-god, lord of
the gods and creator of mankind. Since "Baal" meant properly "lord," the name also appears as a component element
of other divine names, but used alone it referred only to the
great cosmic figure of the storm-god.

It is no easy task to reconstruct the details of the Conquest,
since the extant Israelite tradition is not uniform and our
biblical sources vary considerably. Moreover, there are scarcely
any inscriptions which throw direct light on the time and circumstances of the Israelite invasion; and the results of excavations are ambiguous and sometimes in apparent conflict with
the tradition. However, we are much better off than we were
a generation ago. The progress of excavation and of philologi-
cal interpretation of inscriptions has made it absolutely certain,
in the writer's judgment, that the principal phase of the Conquest must be dated in the second half of the thirteenth century. The destruction of the last Canaanite towns of Tell Beit
Mirsim (probably Debir) and Bethel must be dated in the
thirteenth century. The destruction of the last Canaanite
Lachish is probably to be dated in or about 1220 B.C., immediately before the reference to Israel as a nomadic folk conquered by Egyptian arms on a triumphal stele of Marniptah,
set up in 1219 B.C. At all events, an Egyptian document re-
cording the payment of local tribute in the fourth year of
Marniptah or one of his two ephemeral successors, which was
discovered by Starkey in 1937, requires a date for the burning
of Lachish in 1220 or somewhat later.

The excavation of Hazor by Yigael Yadin in 1955-58 has
enormously enlarged our horizon—not least with regard to the
time of the Israelite occupation.[58] In the Middle and Late
Bronze periods Hazor was a large city by the standards of
those ages, extending over a terrain of about 1000 by 400
meters inside the city wall; the original mound was then occupied by the citadel while the lower city lay north of it, inside the Middle Bronze fortifications. The two uppermost

strata of the lower city correspond archaeologically to the two uppermost Late Bronze levels of the citadel mound; the lower of the two strata in question is dated by its pottery (which includes Late Helladic III A ware) to the late fourteenth or early thirteenth century B.C., so the upper stratum may come down into the middle and latter part of the thirteenth century. In the following Iron Age (twelfth-eleventh centuries) there were two Israelite occupations, both poor towns or villages restricted to the mound proper. The earlier of these two settlements was characterized by the same pottery found by Aharoni in the earliest Israelite settlements elsewhere in Galilee.

The problem of Jericho is quite different. Here we have a Late Bronze mud-brick stratum which was all but completely eroded by wind and rain during the four centuries between the probable date of its destruction by the Israelites and its reoccupation in the time of Ahab. Such phenomena are exceedingly common in the Middle East. The writer has excavated or examined exposed sites of different periods which have left nothing but heavy material, all else being washed or blown away. Henri Frankfort concluded that nearly twenty feet had been eroded from the top of Tell Asmar (Eshnunna) in eastern Babylonia during an abandonment of more than two millennia. Since pottery from the fourteenth-thirteenth centuries B.C. has been found around the foundations of a stone building from about the tenth century B.C., in the lower debris outside the great Middle Bronze battered (sloping) wall, and in the latest tombs of the adjacent Bronze Age cemetery, there can be no doubt that there was a town of this period on the Jericho mound. The situation is probably like that of Tell Beit Mirsim, excavated by the writer, where there was, in general, no special wall built around the town of the fourteenth-thirteenth centuries, but the battered wall of the Middle Bronze Age was cleared of debris and it served as fortification for the Late Bronze Age settlers. Exterior house walls standing above the top of the battered wall would serve as additional defense. In fact, we are told explicitly that this was the situation at Jericho (Josh. 2:15). If there were any doubt about the amount of erosion that took place at Jericho it should be removed by the situation described by Kathleen Kenyon—even the Middle Bronze strata under the Late Bronze settlement were completely eroded in some areas.[59]

The case of Ai is again different. Here we have a Canaanite town called only *Ha'ay*, "The Ruin," in the Joshua narratives, "close to Beth-aven, east of Bethel" (Josh. 7:2). There is only one possibility; Ai was located at the great site of et-Tell, dug by Judith Marquet-Krause in 1933-35. Here she found one of the largest Bronze Age towns yet excavated in Palestine; it was destroyed not later than the twenty-fifth century B.C.[60] and was never again reoccupied except for a much smaller village of the twelfth-eleventh century B.C. Since Bethel and et-Tell are only a mile and a half apart, in a straight line, and the latter lies east-southeast of the former, there can be no possible doubt about the identification. The writer long ago accepted René Dussaud's suggestion that the name of the adjoining town of Beth-aven (Greek *Baithon*) probably preserved the ancient name of "The Ruin," just as has happened innumerable times in the case of other sites (including Jericho itself).[61] Beth-aven is probably the modern Deir Dubwan, half a mile southeast of et-Tell, and two miles in a straight line from Bethel (Beitin). Since the writer has scoured the district in question in all directions, hunting for ancient sites, he can attest the fact that there is no other possible site for Ai than et-Tell. But the excavations carried on at Bethel since 1934 have conclusively proved that there was a sharp break between the last Canaanite occupation in the thirteenth century B.C. and the first Israelite reoccupation in the twelfth century.[62] The Late Bronze remains are of a very well-built and strongly defended Canaanite town, with beautifully built and paved buildings, whereas the Iron Age houses were crudely built and belong to a peasant family culture of characteristically Israelite type. Since the remains of Canaanite Bethel were completely covered by the Israelite town, and the accumulation of soil in the shallow valleys around Bethel had further concealed traces of older Canaanite occupation, it was only natural that the great adjacent Canaanite site of "The Ruin," which was *in* Bethel according to Israelite speech usage, should have been taken to be the immediate precursor of Israelite Bethel. The name "Luz," said in Judg. 1:23 to have been the former name of Bethel, means "hiding place, fastness, stronghold," and was presumably another name of "The Ruin."[63]

Two towns which figure prominently in the narratives of Joshua but which were not destroyed by the Israelites at that time were Shechem and Gibeon. The recent excavations of G. Ernest Wright at Shechem have proved conclusively that there was no destruction between *c.* 1300-1150, and probably not between the early fourteenth century and the early eleventh. Since Shechem was already partly occupied by Hebrews and immediately became the political center of Joshua's activity, this situation was to be expected. Later Israelite tradition knew only of a destruction in the late Patriarchal Age and another in the time of Gideon's son Abimelech. Gibeon has recently been excavated by James B. Pritchard, who has found remains of a fairly important Middle Bronze town, surrounded by a strong wall, and of Israelite occupation in the Iron Age. In Late Bronze times (fourteenth-thirteenth centuries B.C.), there was a much less important occupation on the site, so far attested only by scattered sherds and tombs.[64] This should be expected, since in the fourteenth century Gibeon was in the territory of the city-state of Jerusalem, which was almost certainly the only well-fortified place in its territory. In Josh. 10:1-5 it is the "king" of Jerusalem who is angered by the defection of Gibeon to Israel and who calls on the other princes of the southern hill-country to join him in recovering the town. A later editor (Josh. 10:3) obviously had a somewhat exaggerated notion of the importance of Gibeon at that time, but he was no doubt influenced by the impressive situation of the site and its relative importance in his own time.

Recent efforts to reduce the historical importance of Joshua to a minimum have been unsuccessful.[65] On the other hand, it seems probable that his military feats were somewhat exaggerated by the standard tradition in Joshua, since the capture of Hebron is elsewhere attributed to Caleb and the seizure of Debir (Kirjath-sepher) is credited to Caleb's son-in-law Othniel, the first "judge." However this may be, excavations show that there was only a short interval between the destruction of such Canaanite towns as Debir and Bethel, and their reoccupation by Israel. This means that the Israelite invasion was not a characteristic irruption of nomads, who continued to live in tents for generations after their first invasion. Neither was the Israelite conquest of Canaan a gradual infiltration, as often insisted by modern scholars. The tradition that virtually all Canaanite towns were burned to the ground while their inhabitants and even the cattle were slaughtered is evidently exaggerated, since such towns as Gibeon, Shechem, Hepher, Tirzah and Zaphon were incorporated into the Israelite tribal system. On the other hand, we know from nearly contemporary references that the practice of *herem*, "devoting to destruction," was quite common in that region and period, so it would have been very strange if the wild and warlike Israelites did not follow the custom of the day. Later tradition recognized that the death or flight of part of the Canaanite population had saved Israel from a process of acculturation which might have had disastrous consequences for the new faith.

There can be no doubt that the number of Israelites had swollen enormously since the days of the desert wanderings in the Negeb, south of Canaan, when Israel was too weak even to occupy the little fortresses on the southern fringe of the country. The religion of Moses was a missionary faith with dynamic appeal to the nomadic and seminomadic tribes of that time. After the first great victories over Sihon, converts may well have flocked to join the triumphant standards of the new faith. Among them was the Syrian diviner, Balaam, to whose brief conversion we owe the oracles which have been transmitted to us in fragmentary form in Num. 23-24.[66] There can be little doubt that the same thing happened in western Palestine. The case of the Gibeonites has been recorded by tradition. Far more significant is the fact that the Book of Joshua does not preserve any detailed tradition regarding the conquest of the land of Ephraim and Manasseh, separating Judah from Issachar and Zebulun. Since Shiloh, seat of the Tabernacle, Shechem, traditional meeting place of the first Israelite assembly after the Conquest, and Timnah, to which Joshua himself retired, were all located in this region, the lack of any canonical tradition about the mode of its occupation is very striking indeed. In other and later sources we do find a tradition about the conquest of central Palestine, but all these sources attribute the conquest to the time of Jacob, several centuries earlier.

In the past, allusions in the Hebrew Bible to the early settlement of some tribes in the same districts which they later occupied, have been treated either as coincidences or more often as unwarranted retrojections from the time of the Monarchy. In some cases this is possible, but as an explanation of all passages it falls decidedly short. Note that in Gen. 34 and 48:22 we have explicit statements about the conquest of Shechem in Manasseh by Jacob's sons or by Jacob himself. In I Chron. 7:21-24 (deriving from pre-exilic sources) we have traditions about the occupation of parts of Ephraim in the days of its Patriarch. In Gen. 38 there is an account of the activities of the Patriarch Judah in territory later belonging to Judah. Rachel is said to have been buried either in the Ephraimite (Ephrathite) enclave around Bethlehem or in Benjaminite territory near Ramah; Ephraim was traditionally Rachel's grandson and Benjamin was her son. These scattered indications are greatly amplified in the Book of Jubilees and especially in the Testament of Judah, both probably from about 175 B.C.[67] It is also noteworthy that the list of conquered Canaanite kings in Josh. 12:9-24 contains three towns from the north-central hill-country which are mentioned nowhere in the standard account in Josh. 1-11: Tappuah, Hepher and Tirzah, the latter two later becoming names of clans of Manasseh. In other words, there were very persistent traditions according to which a considerable part of the Hebrew people remained in Palestine and did not go down to Egypt at all.

When these traditions are combined with the increasing evidence for the presence of 'Apiru in considerable numbers in Palestine during the fourteenth century B.C.,[68] it becomes clear that the Hebrew component in the population of western Palestine was relatively much larger than often assumed. This should be expected, since there was no barrier between the African and Asiatic parts of the Egyptian empire (whether Hyksos or Theban) during most of the time between c. 1700 and c. 1300 B.C., except the relatively narrow peninsula of Sinai and the Wall of the Prince along the Egyptian frontier. Since the latter must have lain in ruins much of the time, there was in general no real difficulty in moving from Egypt to Palestine and *vice versa*. In any case, travel was much easier than between Palestine and the Harran region of northwestern Mesopotamia, which kept in close touch during the Patriarchal Age. Even if mass migration was not feasible part of the time, normal movements of donkey and later of mule caravans back and forth between Egypt and Palestine could not fail to keep the Hebrews in both parts of the Empire well informed about happenings among their kindred. It was, accordingly, only natural that most of the Hebrews in Palestine should join the newcomers from Egypt. It would also be natural for men of Judah to seek out relatives in the southern hill-country and for men of Joseph to join their tribal kindred in the central hill-country. Under such circumstances it is not at all necessary to picture the Israelites of Joshua's time as a horde bursting in from the desert into a peaceful Canaanite countryside. War between Canaanite city-states and between Canaanites and Hebrews was an old story in western Palestine; under Joshua's leadership the Hebrews gained the upper hand, occupying much of the hill-country which they had not held previously and adopting the common designation of "Israel."[69]

The names and division of the tribes must have varied considerably more than suggested by the lists which have been preserved, even though no two early lists in the Hebrew Bible are identical. Thus we have variations in the representation of Joseph, which appears as a single tribe and again as two tribes, Ephraim and Manasseh. Furthermore, Manasseh appears as Machir in the Song of Deborah. Levi is sometimes included, sometimes omitted. Benjamin appears with alternative names, *Ben-yamin* (literally "Son of the South") [70] and *Ben-oni* (literally "Inhabitant of Beth-aven") .[71] Since most of the tribal names are of Middle Bronze Age type, and a number have been discovered in sources from the early second millennium B.C., they must, as a rule, have been in use since Patriarchal times. In any event, it usually requires centuries for tribes and clans to develop, so it is quite incredible that the tribal structure arose in Palestine after the Conquest, as is sometimes supposed. The writer's own view is that the twelve-fold division dates from the traditional separation of the mixed mob of refugees who fled from Egypt into *alafim* ("clans," also "thousands") by Moses on Jethro's advice (Ex. 18). Needless to say, names were needed for the new *alafim*, so they were presumably selected from tribal groups which were particularly well represented in the new entities. This explanation can naturally not be proved, but it accounts for the presence of the old tribal names, handed down in both Egypt and Palestine, or in one of them, as well as for the heterogeneous composition of the refugees, also well attested in our tradition. This development can be paralleled all over the world in comparable situations.

TRIBAL RULE
AND CHARISMATIC LEADERS

IV

An impartial observer of the early twelfth century B.C. would probably have said that everything was against the success of the Israelite experiment. At that time Israel was still a heterogeneous amalgam of elements of very different origins, and the memory of their mixed background as state serfs in Egypt and 'Apiru caravaneers and freebooters in Palestine was still vivid. The peoples of Canaan were very conscious of aristocracy and old lineage, but the Israelites had neither a class system (except in so far as the Aaronids and the children of clan leaders represented class) nor aristocratic ancestry. Among the Israelites there were few craftsmen and scant respect for the amenities of civilization: the archaeologist can scarcely be faced with a greater contrast than that between the well-built and well-drained patrician houses of the last Canaanite Bethel and the rustic constructions and lack of drainage characteristic of all three of the earliest Israelite periods of building. The early religion of Israel had little art and probably little or no music. Against the ancient liturgy of Canaanite temples and their elaborately organized personnel appeared in sharp contrast the aesthetic barrenness of the early cult of Yahweh. Against the rich mythology and the dramatic ritual of Canaanite religion stood out the lonely figure of the desert God, without mythology and virtually without ritual. Against the emotional ecstasy of orgiastic Canaanite rites there came no answering echo from the stern code of Israelite morality. Where the Canaanites were sophisticated the Israelites were harsh with the cruel simplicity of nomads; where the Canaanites gloated in sadistic glee the Israelites turned away in shocked reaction against the brutalities of an oversophisticated culture.[72]

In spite of the initial successes of the Israelites between c.

1250 and 1200 B.C., they could scarcely have continued to expand if it had not been for the period of Egyptian decline which followed the death of Marniptah about 1215. For over a decade three weak rulers held the façade of empire together, but the Egyptian dependencies, extremely restive under Marniptah, must have broken away almost entirely from their allegiance to Pharaoh. After this decade Egypt fell into a state of anarchy for "many years," as vividly portrayed in the preamble to the famous Papyrus Harris; an unnamed Syrian finally made himself chief, but no contemporary monuments elucidate the episode. It was not until c. 1180 B.C. that an energetic young king, Rameses III, was able to undertake the recovery of the Asiatic empire of Egypt. Thanks to this breathing spell the Israelites were able to establish themselves firmly in the hill-country of western Palestine, from Kedesh in northern Naphtali to Debir in southwestern Judah, and from central Hauran to the Arnon in eastern Palestine (Trans-Jordan). Among territory then held and subsequently lost must be counted in particular the region north of the Arnon, which was taken by the Moabites, the land of Bashan, which was occupied by the Arameans, and at least part of the Plain of Sharon, seized by the Sea Peoples. As a result of these and other losses, the tribes of Reuben, Manasseh, Dan, Asher, and Simeon were greatly reduced in power and influence. It was not until the time of David that the lost territory was regained, and much of it was lost again within a century.

The Israelite confederation of the period of the Judges was in some ways a true amphictyony, as recognized especially by Albrecht Alt and Martin Noth.[73] Like Greek and Italic amphictyonies of a somewhat later period, it consisted of a federation of distinct tribes, grouped around a central sanctuary, which exercised a strong cohesive force, unifying the tribes in religion and politics, as well as to some extent also in language and customs. The amphictyonic confederation of Israel differed widely in one respect from the constitutions of the Greek and Italic amphictyonies. So far as we know, none of these states had anything comparable to the covenant between the God of Israel and His people, which we can now trace back archaeologically—in agreement with biblical tradition—to the time of Abraham. The covenant at Sinai was essentially religious in character, and we know little about its political aspects. On the other hand, the covenant between God and Israel solemnized by Joshua at Shechem (Josh. 24) was both religious and political. G. E. Mendenhall has shown that the covenant of Joshua has almost the same structure as the suzerainty treaties of the Hittite kings of the fourteenth-thirteenth centuries with vassal rulers of Anatolia, Syria and Mesopotamia.[74] This common structure includes the introductory preamble, the historical prologue, the stipulations (greatly reduced in number), a much modified oath formula, mention of witnesses, and a specific reference to the deposit of the text of the treaty in the sanctuary. There are, of course, notable differences which are required by the change from polytheism to monotheism and from an imperial power to a confederation of tribes in the process of settling down. But the parallels in structure cannot be dismissed lightly, especially as there are greater differences in structure between the extant cuneiform treaties of the second millennium and the Assyrian and Aramean treaties of the eighth-seventh centuries B.C. These parallels at the very least establish the antiquity of the covenant of Joshua, which is also perhaps attested by the curses and blessings of Deut. 27-28, definitely associated by tradition with Shechem and the time of Joshua. The curses, which form a characteristic element of the Hittite treaties, are not mentioned in Josh. 24.

Israel possessed an unusually powerful centripetal force in the Mosaic tradition. On the other hand, strong centrifugal forces were operating to break up the federation. In the first place, Israelite territory was not well suited geographically to form a political unit. Galilee was separated from Manasseh and Ephraim by the broad Plain of Jezreel, controlled by Canaanite chariotry, against which the footmen of Israel were as helpless as modern infantry against tanks. Nor were relations between Judah and Ephraim any too well knit, though the usual view that they were separated by a chain of Canaanite fortresses was probably not true during most of our period. The barrier of the Jordan Valley was not serious; it was more important that the problems and dangers which faced the tribes of Trans-Jordan were very different from those which confronted their kinsmen in western Palestine.[75] Even more of a barrier than these obvious geographical interruptions was the fact that travel from north to south was generally restricted to the narrow ridge separating the watershed of the Mediterranean from that of the Jordan: a shift of two or three miles to the east or west of this ridge meant, as a rule, that the transverse valleys and gorges became twice as difficult to cross. Moreover, these geographical barriers favored cantonization, which perpetuated or created boundaries between dialects, customs and political orientation.

The early missionary drive which dominated Israel under Moses and Joshua soon began to weaken, though several traditions recorded in Judges and Samuel show that it did not die out entirely. Pre-Mosaic beliefs and practices emerged, and the native paganism of Canaanite and Hebrew groups which had been absorbed only partially into the Israelite confederation returned to favor. The conflict between Yahweh and Baal gradually grew in popular consciousness; it is first concretely stated in the surviving tradition of Gideon, about a century or more after the Conquest. It is still unclear to what extent Baal was identified with Yahweh in the period of the Judges, but the frequency of Baal names among the families of both Saul and David (see below) makes it appear likely that syncretism between Yahweh and Baal was already favored in certain circles.

The centrifugal process was checked by foreign aggression rather than by internal evolution toward more stable political forms. Of all threats from the outside the most formidable was that of the Philistines, who invaded Palestine by sea and land about 1175-1170 B.C., half a century after the climax of the Israelite invasion. In league with other seafaring peoples from the northern shores of the Mediterranean they overwhelmed the resistance of the Hittites and Canaanites, and invaded Egypt itself before they were defeated. The Egyptian king made a virtue of necessity, however, allowing the Sea Peoples to establish themselves along the shores of Palestine from Gaza to Dor and probably still farther north.[76] Further strengthened by immigration across the Mediterranean, the

Sea Peoples maintained close ties with Aegean lands for centuries. After the middle of the twelfth century their influence began to penetrate inland, as we know from pottery finds in the towns of the Judahite Shephelah (low hill-country).[77] The report of the Egyptian envoy Wen-amun, c. 1060 B.C., shows that they were then competing actively with the Canaanite cities of Phoenicia for control of the lucrative sea trade.[78] About the middle of the eleventh century the Philistines defeated Israel at the battle of Ebenezer and captured the Ark. Excavations indicate that the Philistines also overran and destroyed many towns in Judah and Ephraim, including Debir, Beth-zur, Shiloh.[79] The hegemony over Palestine set up at that time did not end until the victories of Saul and especially of David.

In northern Palestine the greatest threat was posed by the strongly fortified Canaanite towns which had escaped destruction, such as Megiddo and Taanach on the southwestern edge of Esdraelon, Accho and Achshaph in the plain of Acre. Here too there was a triangular situation, with the Sea Peoples pressing inland against both Canaan and Israel while these latter were struggling with one another for the upper hand. The Song of Deborah in Judg. 5 gives a vivid firsthand account of a battle which must have been rather decisive; the prose narrative which precedes it (Judg. 3:31-34:24) is based on the Song, which it sometimes misunderstands; but there are additional data derived from tradition which help us to reconstruct the situation. Yadin's excavation of Hazor has clarified the situation considerably, since we now know that Hazor had been destroyed before the Philistine invasion, whereas the battle of Taanach, celebrated in the Song of Deborah, was not fought until after the Philistine invasion.[80] Sisera's name is not Canaanite, but may well have belonged to one of the Sea Peoples.[81] The scene of the battle between the North-Israelite tribal contingents and the army of the Canaanite "kings," is placed in the Song "at Taanach by the Waters of Megiddo." It has long since been recognized that this contemporary description of the battlefield would have been completely unintelligible unless Megiddo then lay in ruins. Excavations at Taanach and Megiddo have shown that there were only a few periods in which both flourished simultaneously. After all, they were only about five miles apart in a straight line! Megiddo was actually abandoned between the destruction of the town of Stratum VII and the occupation by the Israelites in Stratum VI, *i.e.*, between a date in the third quarter of the twelfth century (1150-1125) and a date somewhere in the first half of the eleventh century B.C.[82] It is virtually certain that the battle took place when the army of Sisera was emerging from the famous 'Ara Pass into the little plain south of Megiddo, where the stream called *Qina* in the Annals of Tuthmosis III starts. Possibly Canaanite contingents from the plains of Esdraelon and Acre were due to meet Sisera on the plain below Taanach, where their chariotry would have a tremendous advantage over the Israelite footmen. In any event, sound strategy on the part of the Israelite leader, together with a cloudburst which produced a flash flood in the Kishon and its southern tributary streams, proved disastrous to Sisera and his Canaanite allies.[83]

In Trans-Jordan there was aggression from several directions, and the waves of invasion which broke against it often flowed over into western Palestine, leaving no part of Israel secure from attack. First, somewhere in the twelfth century, came a successful Moabite invasion and occupation, brought to an end by a bold stroke carried out by a Benjaminite named Ehud. Ehud is the first of the judges whose figure stands out with some clarity against the background of Israelite heroic saga. Like most of the subsequent "judges" (*shophetim*) of this period whose names are recorded in the Bible, Ehud obtained the title, not by magisterial functioning in a court, but by deeds of extraordinary martial prowess. Most of these judges were not magistrates, but military heroes and successful commanders of armies; they were respected and obeyed by their fellow countrymen, regardless of their tribal affiliation and their social origin, because they were believed to possess some special outpouring of the spirit of God which made them superior in valor and wisdom to the common man. Leaders of this type have been happily called "charismatic leaders" by Max Weber and Albrecht Alt.[84] It is probable that the Israelites adopted the use of the word *shophet* in this sense from their Canaanite precursors, since the same term appears in the sense of "prince" in earlier Canaanite mythology and it was still used in Carthage, centuries later, to designate the heads of the state. There can be no doubt, moreover, that there was an inner-Israelite development of the charismatic associations of judgeship. Several of the minor judges, of whom nothing is recorded but their names and the number of years during which they functioned, evidently owed their distinction to their success as intertribal arbitrators.[85] As among the nomadic and semi-nomadic Arabs of recent times, wisdom and impartiality in making decisions according to tribal customary law were quite enough to spread the fame of a popular arbitrator, to whom men might come scores of miles for arbitration of knotty cases. In the raw semi-sedentary culture of Israel in the days of the Judges, respected arbitrators and interpreters of tribal law played a highly important role in restricting lawlessness and blood feuds. It was thus no light honor when a successful military leader or a popular hero was consulted by his followers, for whom physical prowess and shrewdness in strategy carried social prestige and reputation for wisdom.

Late in the twelfth century the newly settled tribes of Israel were struck by an avalanche from the Syrian Desert which all but overwhelmed them. This was the first irruption of camel-riding nomads into the Fertile Crescent of which we have any historical record. Domesticated camels were so rare in early times that they never appear in our contemporary records and monuments in the earlier centuries of the second millennium.[86] Not long before our time, however, the wild tribes of inner Arabia had learned how to ride the camel over long distances and to surprise wholly unsuspecting victims asleep in remote encampments. Thus the Bedouin razzia came into existence. Year after year the wild Arab hordes poured over Palestine, forcing the Israelites into the mountains and forests, and plundering their crops and their livestock. Tradition described the hordes as "Midian and Amalek and the Bne Qedem" (Judg. 6:3). Had their depredations been allowed to continue unchecked, Israel would have been displaced from Canaan before it had completed a century and a half of occupation. Thanks to the valor and shrewdness of a man of western Manasseh named Jerubbaal (Gideon) this great danger was averted, and Palestine was saved from further Arab inundation for over four centuries. Moreover, Gideon was not only a successful charismatic leader; he was also a militant propagandist for the God of Israel, carrying the war against Baalism into the camp of the followers of Baal. The fact that his own personal name was formed with "Baal" while that of his father Joash was formed with "Yahweh" vividly illustrates the confused religious situation prevailing at that time in north-central Israel.

About the middle of the eleventh century or a little later, the Philistines, after a century of desultory conflict and increasing pressure on southern Israel, invaded the highlands of Ephraim in force and destroyed Shiloh, as demonstrated by the Danish excavations there. As we have noted above, this victory was followed by the destruction of other Israelite towns, and probably cost Israel much of the material wealth which it had accumulated during the preceding generation. The burning of Shiloh and loss of the Ark left the Israelite amphictyony without a central sanctuary, thus gravely endangering its stability. By their master stroke the Philistines might have made themselves permanent lords of Palestine had it not been for the emergence of Samuel not long afterwards. His great popular reputation as judge and diviner bridged the gap between the old charismatic and the new prophetic age; his early association with the high priest, Eli, bridged another gap between the amphictyony and the Monarchy.

The role of Samuel in the triumph of Mosaic ideals and in the successful transition from tribal confederation to centralized monarchy, has not been understood until recently. In fact, the writer was completely in the dark himself until 1958, when O. Eissfeldt published his brilliant monograph on the date and background of Deut. 32.[87] Several then very recent discoveries among the Dead Sea Scrolls and the Sefire treaties cleared up important points of detail, and the historical picture came rapidly into focus.[88] As a result of these advances, the differences in emphasis which we find in the narratives of Samuel no longer appear as hopeless contradictions, but rather as essential contributions to the total historical picture. In other words, we have in the traditions about Samuel material for a wider historical perspective than we perhaps find in any other critical phase of the history of ancient Israel. The fidelity with which different traditions reproduced divergent facets of the historical situation cannot be equalled elsewhere in the Hebrew Bible, where we usually find much elimination of unconventional points of view (as in the standardized picture of Joshua's conquest).

We have four kinds of discrepancies, real or superficial: (1) Samuel appears both as an Ephraimite of the clan of Zuph and as a Levite from a family of singers (I Sam. 1:1 and I Chron. 6:16-43); (2) he was judge over all Israel, holding power until the accession of Saul, but he is also described, toward the end of his tenure, as an obscure diviner, unknown to Saul (who lived only a few miles away); (3) he is said to have routed the Philistines and to have freed Israel from them "all his days," but later Israel is said to have remained under Philistine domination down into the time of Saul; (4) he was hostile to the establishment of the monarchy, but he changed his mind and favored it, anointing Saul and presiding over his public choice as monarch.

These seeming discrepancies are reduced to proper focus by the recent discoveries referred to above. In the first place, it is now certain that early tradition considered Samuel as a *nazir*, that is, as a person vowed to lifelong service of God and pledged never to shave his hair or beard and never to drink alcoholic beverages. Though this is nowhere stated in the extant Hebrew or Greek Bibles, it appears in an early recension of I Sam. found in Cave IV at Qumran,[89] as well as in the Hebrew recension of Ben Sira (Ecclesiasticus) recovered since 1897 from the Ezra Synagogue in Cairo.[90] It is also affirmed explicitly in the Mishnah (though there was an opposing view) and presupposed by the reference in the Hebrew Bible to the inviolability of Samuel's hair and beard (I Sam. 1:11), to which the Greek Bible adds abstinence from alcoholic beverages. But a *nazir*, pledged from childhood to divine service in the Tabernacle at Shiloh, performed Levitic obligations and may well have been considered as a Levite. His connection with Levitic singers is not surprising, in view of the well-attested use of instrumental music in his prophetic gatherings. Samuel's role in the Israelite commonwealth must have been at least as complex as that of some other leading "judges." He was a *shophet* who arbitrated between the tribes and clans, a *ro'eh*, "diviner," a *nabi*, "one specially called by God." He led his people against the Philistines, but was later permitted by the latter to continue as "judge," following a practice widespread in all ages, of ruling a subject people through a leader of its own choice. His role as involuntary king-maker will be discussed below.

By far the most important aspect of Samuel's career was his break with the Elide priesthood and his replacement—in whole or in part—of the priestly hierarchy by the ecstatic prophets. All through later Judeo-Christian history we find such more or less periodic replacements—wholly or partly—of the established priesthood, or clergy, or rabbinate by new spiritual leaders from the ranks of the laity.[91] Such repeated transformations seem to have been essential to the success of a spiritual and ethical structure built on a basis of strict monotheism with a constitution founded on the covenant principle. This principle could not be maintained without constant reformation, and each reformation demanded partial or complete change in leadership. Sometimes, as in later Judah or in the Catholic Church since the Counter-Reformation, a balanced spiritual leadership has been achieved by balancing priests against prophets, or a secular hierarchy against the religious orders and congregations. Usually, one class replaces another entirely or almost entirely. We may safely suppose that this was Samuel's original intention. In the first place, tradition emphasizes the wickedness of the Elide priesthood and the justice of divine punishment; this is not only stressed in the Book of Samuel, but also in Psalm 78 and probably in Deut. 32. Nowhere is Samuel represented, after the destruction of the Tabernacle, as taking the least interest in priesthood, Tabernacle, or Ark. On the contrary, he is described as presiding over meetings of the ecstatic prophets and as forwarding the movement[92] in other ways. When Saul quarrels with Samuel, Saul takes the side of the priests, whom he establishes in a new home near his own residence.

It seems virtually certain to the writer that Eissfeldt is correct in attributing Deut. 32 to the time of Samuel, about the middle of the eleventh century B.C. Its contents are throughout archaic, though it is more recent in style than the Song of Miriam, the Oracles of Balaam or the Song of Deborah. There is nowhere any hint that the Monarchy had been established, though in the related Song of Hannah the role of Saul (or David) is presupposed, and in the tenth-century Psalm 78, which supplements Deut. 32, David appears explicitly. Our understanding of Deut. 32 has been greatly enlarged by the finds in Cave IV of Qumran, which make the archaism of the Song of Moses clearer than ever before.[93] In this composition we not only see the monotheism of Israel groping for more radical formulation; we also observe the process of demythologizing ancient myths, without the artificial archaism characteristic of some late compositions. For example, in Deut. 32:8 f. we may now render (following the Greek and Qumran) :

> When the Most High distributed allotments,
>> when He separated the children of man,
> He set the borders of the peoples
>> like the number of sons of God;
> But Yahweh's portion is His people,
>> Jacob is His allotted domain!

Here the Most High is, of course, identical with Yahweh, but in the underlying ethnogonic myth two gods were presumably involved. The term "sons of God" (*bene El*) referred in Canaanite to the seventy sons of El and his consort, Asherah; they were, in other words, the gods. In monotheistic Israel they became the tutelary angels of the seventy nations, a concept which survived even into Rabbinic times, though it was not necessarily accepted in earlier normative Yahwism. The intransigent monotheism of the author of our poem is made all the more vivid by his archaic imagery.

While we have no good reason to attribute the composition of Deut. 32 to Samuel, it may well have been composed by a member of his immediate circle. It shared with the Song of Miriam in Ex. 15 the distinction of being one of the two most sacred hymns in the Hebrew Bible. Both were transmitted in stichometric form, that is, with verse units separated by spaces. Its remarkable state of preservation must be due to the fact that its language was familiar to every pious Israelite. The style points to a date after the Blessing of Moses but before the Blessing of Jacob (in its extant form). While it does not refer to Moses explicitly like the Blessing of Moses, there are a number of allusions which obviously suggested Mosaic authorship of an otherwise anonymous poem. Without the figure of Samuel and the theological content of Deut. 32, it is difficult to imagine the Prophetic movement in Israel, or the Deuteronomic literature which grew out of the theological point of view of the Prophets.[94] When Jeremiah declared (15:1), "And Yahweh said to me, 'Even if Moses and Samuel stood before me (on the people's behalf), I should not take the side of this people'," Samuel obviously represents the Prophets, just as Moses is the spokesman of the priestly order.

In the course of two centuries there had been great development in the material civilization and social organization of Israel, in spite of repeated blows from outside, some of them crushing in their impact. Most of the destroyed Canaanite towns had been reoccupied, and these towns became foci of agricultural clans grouped in patriarchally organized families. The average population of the major towns was much smaller than in Canaanite times, and open spaces were used for sheepfolds and grain pits. Characteristic of the age, at least in places like Debir, Beth-shemesh and Bethel, were large rustic houses, with numerous rooms on the ground floor around an open courtyard, and other rooms upstairs. Construction and character of furnishings prove conclusively that these large houses were not aristocratic mansions, like the Canaanite buildings whose place they sometimes take, but were occupied by several smaller families, grouped around a patriarchal head. Moreover, thanks to the extremely rapid diffusion of the art of building cisterns, introduced not long before the end of the Canaanite occupation (see above), it had become possible to build new towns and villages on sites far from any spring or running stream. And so hundreds of new settlements had arisen where no Canaanite settlement had ever been; illustrations from the neighborhood of Jerusalem are Gibeah, Ramah, Geba, Michmas—to mention only a few names of towns known to go back to the period before Samuel. Considerable areas of woodland, both east and west of the Jordan, had been cleared; vast numbers of vines and olive trees had been planted.

Moreover, commerce was fast returning to the place it held under the Canaanites; in some respects it probably surpassed any previous record in Palestine. Camel caravans were already providing new means of transporting the wares of the desert into Palestine, not to mention the tremendous new possibilities which they provided for cheap transport over greater distances. The rapid growth of the little country of Ammon, on the very edge of the desert east of Gilead, after the time of the Conquest, in which it played no role, until it was able to threaten Israel repeatedly in the course of the eleventh century, illustrates what the camel trade already meant at this time.[95] In the Mediterranean sea trade was rapidly expanding after the interruption created by the movements of the Sea Peoples in the late thirteenth and twelfth centuries. The Report of Wen-amun, already mentioned above, vividly illustrates the rapid expansion of merchant shipping, organized in large corporations for better protection against pirates and raiders.[96] The Song of Deborah mentions the active maritime part played by members of the tribes of Dan and Asher. By the end of the eleventh century, pottery imported from Cyprus appears again in Israelite sites, after a long interruption during which exceedingly little imported ware (except Philistine) is found.

The increase in wealth, combined with the menace of the Philistines, made a more stable political organization imperative. Gideon's son Abimelech headed a Canaanite reaction at Shechem, and made himself briefly "king." Samuel attempted to establish the succession of "judges" on a stable basis by appointing his own sons to that office. Both efforts, like others which were soon forgotten, were failures: Abimelech proved to be a bloody tyrant and was ignominiously killed by a woman; Samuel's sons were corrupt in the administration of justice and became targets for the clamor of the people. The way was thus opened for a new step in the political evolution of Israel.

This step was the appointment of a charismatic figure as

nagid, "leader," of Israel for life. In three passages referring to Saul we note that Samuel anointed him as *nagid,* not as *melekh,* "king," over Israel. Similarly, in four other passages referring to David, he was anointed as *nagid,* not as *melekh.* The word *nagid* undoubtedly meant "leader, commander," like later Aramaic *negida* and *nagoda;* it already had this meaning in the ¯Sefire Treaties from *c.* 750 B.C.[97] Much recent discussion of the meaning of *nagid* has been vitiated by efforts to discover new senses, otherwise not documented. Actually, the use of *nagid* in the sense of charismatic leader was never really forgotten in Israel; it has recently come to light in Ben Sira 46:13 and in the Hebrew recension of Psalm 151 (of the Greek Bible) from Qumran Cave XI.[98] The device by which Samuel persuaded the people to elect a popular leader for life instead of a king who might found a dynasty, could scarcely be successful, in view of human nature, but it did bridge the gap between a charismatic and a monarchical constitution. In Northern Israel the principle seems to have remained alive until the end of the kingdom, but in Judah the prestige of the House of David canceled it. We may be sure that in practice the term *melekh* began to be applied to the new leader as soon as he was installed—for was not every Canaanite princeling a "king"?

THE UNITED MONARCHY

V

A popular hero, Saul, was proclaimed *nagid* ("leader") in spite of the initial opposition of Samuel. At the very beginning of his reign he won decisive victories over the Ammonites, Philistines and Amalekites, thus freeing Israel from immediate danger on all sides of the country. His jealous, tyrannical nature, amply illustrated by tradition, could not brook opposition, and so he was gradually forced into hostility toward every actual or potential rival for power. Early in his reign came the break with Samuel, followed shortly afterward by the quarrel with David, his son-in-law and already a popular hero on his own account. Tradition recalled these dramatic personal relationships and illustrated them vividly by anecdotes which throw a bright light on the personalities involved; tradition failed to consider underlying tendencies and policies. The conflict between Saul and David was apparently at bottom little more than a contest for popular favor and power between two charismatic leaders, but the bitterness between Samuel and Saul had a much broader base. There is no hint in our sources that Samuel took any action with regard to restoration of the tabernacle of Shiloh, and the Ark remained at Kirjath-jearim until well along in the reign of David. Saul, however, collected the surviving Elides and installed them at Nob, less than an hour's walk to the southeast of Gibeah, Saul's own residence. Here was erected some kind of structure to house the sacred objects and rites; the Ark might also have been brought here, in spite of the superstitious awe in which it was held by the people, if there had been time to plan for the transfer. As it was, we may safely infer that Saul's action had two purposes, first to strengthen his hand against Samuel, second to give him direct personal control of the high-priestly family, with its strong traditional and symbolic meaning to Israel. When Saul ordered the slaughter of all the Elides, in a fit of jealous rage because they had assisted David, he broke with orthodox Yahwism completely. His earlier piety, illustrated by the tradition that he suppressed witchcraft and necromancy in Israel (I Sam. 28:3), may even have been replaced by outright syncretism. It is in any case a curious fact that, while his eldest son was called Jonathan, a name formed with "Yahweh," names formed with "Baal" occur at least three times among the younger Saulides. Saul may have been moved by considerations of political expediency in thus favoring Baalism, which was much more strongly entrenched in the north than in the south. At all events, he was sufficiently interested in maintaining control over the northern territories of Israel to meet his death in a hopeless battle to defend the Esdraelon pass against a powerful Philistine army (c. 1000 B.C.).

The writer's excavation of the remains of Saul's fortress at Gibeah illustrates the rustic simplicity of his court better than anything else can do.[99] Though strongly constructed, the fortress walls were built of hammer-dressed masonry, and its contents were extremely simple. It is probable that the fortress was originally constructed by the Philistines as one of a chain (I Sam. 10:5) and was adapted by Saul for his own purpose. Tradition makes clear that Saul never had a standing army of more than nominal strength, so he remained at the mercy of tribal institutions and customs throughout his reign. Under such circumstances he could win great victories over the semi-nomadic Ammonites and Amalekites, but he was quite unable to make any real headway against so solidly organized a confederation as the Philistine pentapolis.

The death of Saul and his sons at the disastrous battle of Gilboa opened the way for David's brilliant career. Thanks to his deeds of heroism and to his singular personal charm, attested by all relevant traditions, David enjoyed the widest popular favor, scarcely dimmed by his long service under the Philistine Achish, tyrant of Gath. He was thus as striking a charismatic figure as any in earlier Israelite history. Moreover, David had unusual gifts of mind. He was celebrated by Israelite tradition as a musician, and there can be no reasonable doubt as to the importance of his own direct and indirect contributions to Hebrew music and poetry, on which archaeological finds have recently cast very interesting light.[100] As general and statesman he was also a distinguished figure.

During David's seven-year reign in Hebron he consolidated his power and apparently waged successful war against the Philistines. Recent archaeological research strongly suggests that the casemated walls of Debir and Beth-shemesh were built by David as part of a line of defense against the Philistines.[101] After the assassination of Saul's youngest son, Esh-baal (Ish-bosheth),[102] the heads of the northern tribes invited him to become king of reunited Israel. His own and his predecessor's experience with the fickleness of tribal support seems directly responsible for his decision to establish his new capital at a non-Israelite site on the borders of the two reunited halves of his kingdom; a brief and obscure siege was sufficient to reduce Jerusalem, thenceforward called officially "City of David." Jerusalem was quite outside of the Israelite tribal system; it owed allegiance only to the king, and it became peopled largely by his personal retainers, who had abandoned their original allegiances and were legally "slaves of the king," a term used regularly by the Israelites and their neighbors in the sense of "royal officials." This act of David was sheer political genius.[103]

Having established his court at Jerusalem, David next took measures to attach the amphictyonic tradition to himself by moving the few survivors of the Nob massacre to the city, where he erected a tabernacle in which the Ark, venerated ancient symbol of Israel's faith, was presently installed. According to tradition, David set in motion elaborate plans for building a temple on the summit of the hill overlooking Jerusalem from the north, which he had acquired from its Jebusite owner. However this may be, there can be no reasonable doubt that tradition was essentially correct in attributing to David far-reaching modifications and improvements in the organization of divine worship, especially in the orchestral system.[104] Moreover, examination of the list of Levitic cities, according to which four places in each tribe were designated for the residence of priests and Levites, makes it certain that—unless the

original list was a late fiction, for which it is extremely hard
to find plausible grounds—it must go back to the latter part of
David's reign (or the very beginning of the reign of Solomon),
since it was only then that the towns in question were all part
of Israel, according to historical and archaeological indications,
and only then that the political background was suitable.[105] By
distributing the priests and Levites over the country, David
weakened them politically at the same time that he con-
tributed to the spread of normative Yahwism.[106]

Similar considerations make it highly probable that the six
cities of refuge, all of which were included among the Levitic
cities, were instituted in or immediately after the reign of
David.[107] This institution can have been intended only as part
of a campaign to suppress the time-honored practice of blood
revenge, with the resulting vendettas which have repeatedly
brought total destruction to groups and communities in the
tribal history of Palestine, whether under Canaanites, Israelites or Arabs. No stable government can coexist with blood
feuds. David's famous census was another phase of his struggle
to restrict the autonomy of the tribes by placing them under a
bureaucratic administration answerable only to the crown.
The redivision of Israel into new districts distinct in large part
from the old tribal territories was carried into effect by Solomon, presumably in accordance with a plan initiated by his
father.

As a result of David's brilliant victories over the Edomites,
Moabites, Ammonites, Arameans and Philistines, he extended
the nominal boundaries of Israel as far as central Syria in the
northwest and the Euphrates Valley in the northeast.[108] The
entire coast from Carmel to south of Joppa became Israelite,
and the Philistines were reduced to paying tribute. Since much
of the booty and probably all the tribute were turned in to the
royal coffers, the crown became immensely wealthy. These extensive resources were used partly to support a steadily increasing army of mercenary troops and royal officials, all of whom
(see above) owed personal allegiance only to the king. The
functionaries of the king were organized according to
models set by the Egyptian bureaucratic system, whether bor-

rowed directly or through Canaanite (Phoenician) intermediation.[109]

David failed signally in regulating the succession to the throne, and thus in stabilizing royal institutions in Israel. The revolt of Absalom was possible only in a society where the charismatic principle of leadership was still dominant and where an accepted dynastic principle had not yet taken root. Around Absalom gathered all the dissatisfied elements of Israel: early friends and relatives of David who were bitter because of lack of success at court; members or adherents of the house of Saul; non-Judahite Israelites who disliked the most-favored place of Judah in David's organization of the state. Even on David's deathbed an insurrection broke out, attempting to displace the palace favorite, Solomon, by the fourth son of the king, Adonijah. The attempt to crown Adonijah proved abortive, but it was a bad portent for the future unity of Israel.

Solomon's long reign (c. 961-922 B.C.) [110] has always been justly celebrated as the culmination of Israelite material history. Thanks to his inherited wealth and power, as well as to his own shrewdness in taking advantage of favorable economic circumstances, he created an impression on his contemporaries which made him a central figure of saga and legend. Among hundreds of millions of Moslems the riches and wisdom of Suleiman, who reigned over all men and jinn, still dominate story and proverb. The political setting of the age was singularly favorable: Egypt, under the last feeble rulers of the Tanite Dynasty, was in no position to interfere in Asia; Assyria, under the fainéant Tiglath-pileser II (966-935 B.C.),[111] was at one of the lowest points reached in a long history; the new Sidonian state with its capital at Tyre was absorbed in sea trade and commercial expansion;[112] the Arameans had been roundly defeated by David, though they began to recover during Solomon's reign. It was, therefore, quite unnecessary for Solomon to undertake any serious military operations. As a warning against would-be aggressors he established a powerful standing army, consisting mainly of chariotry, which his father had still refused to employ. The figures in Kings and

Chronicles are conflicting, but the most probable ones attribute to him 1,400 chariots, 4,000 stalls for the chariot horses, and some 12,000 horses. Even allowing for a certain amount of exaggeration, this represented a potent force, roughly equivalent to the amount of chariotry thrown by Hadad-ezer of Damascus against Shalmaneser III at the battle of Qarqar a century later. One of the chariot cities which Solomon rebuilt has been excavated; the excavators of Megiddo have estimated that in the following century there were some 450 well-built stalls for horses in that site alone.

With this assurance against foreign interference, Solomon could turn his attention to the marvelous opportunities for trade and development of the arts of civilization that were then opening up. Our sources describe commerce with Phoenicia, Egypt, South Arabia and adjacent regions, as well as with Hittite North Syria and Cilicia. By intermarriage with Egypt he became an ally of that country. He entered into close partnership with Hiram of Tyre (969-936 B.C.) in organizing elaborate trading expeditions on the Red Sea and the Indian Ocean, possibly also in the Mediterranean. At that time Phoenician commercial expansion was at its height, and trading colonies were established at least as far west as Sardinia (Tarshish).[113] An essential part of Phoenician colonial activity was then devoted to mining, especially in the rich copper deposits of Cyprus and Sardinia. We do not yet know definitely whether Phoenician expansion had reached southern Spain as early as Hiram's time, though it does not seem impossible. We do know, however, that the name Tarshish ("Refinery"?)[114] was applied in the following century to Nora in southern Sardinia. Thanks to Phoenician collaboration, Solomon constructed copper refineries at Ezion-geber at the northern end of the Red Sea (Gulf of 'Aqabah), where they have been recently excavated by Nelson Glueck.[115] The copper for these refineries (as well as for the copper works mentioned in I Kings 7:45) came from recently discovered copper mines in the Ghor, both south and north of the Dead Sea. No less significant than Solomon's partnership with the Phoenicians was his commercial relationship to "all the kings of the Arabs," including the famous queen of Sheba, which country here makes its first appearance in recorded history. At this time caravan trade in the desert was being revolutionized by the rapid development of the use of domesticated camels for long hauls. Solomon may well have been the first important ruler to exploit this new source of wealth.

With these new means at his disposal Solomon launched out into an elaborate series of building operations. We are well acquainted with the construction of the Temple and royal palace, thanks to the detailed—though often obscure—description in I Kings; the fortification of Gezer, Megiddo and Hazor has been confirmed by excavation, and we have already alluded to the Megiddo stables and the refineries of Ezion-geber (which are not mentioned in our literary sources). Throughout Phoenician influence is dominant—in the plan of palace and Temple; in the details of hewing, laying courses and quoin construction which characterize Solomonic masonry in sharpest contrast to the masonry of Saul and David; in proto-Aeolic pilaster capitals and other details of architectural ornamentation.[116] All of this cost a great deal, both in treasure and in labor. Solomon reduced the recently conquered Canaanites of Esdraelon, the coastal plain and the outlying districts of Galilee to state slavery (*mas 'obed*).[117] He also presumably forced the conquered states of Trans-Jordan (Edom, Moab and Ammon) to furnish state slaves. Since, however, these sources of cheap labor proved inadequate, he went so far as to resort to the corvée (*mas*) to enlist free Israelites in work battalions, alternating between a month in Lebanon and two months at home. If the recorded number of 30,000 Israelite conscripts is correct, it would constitute a drain on the population roughly equivalent to a draft of 6,000,000 Americans in 1960.[118] It is scarcely probable, however, that even Solomon dared employ this corvée for anything but the construction of the Temple and other buildings of common interest to all.

Solomon continued policies inaugurated apparently by David, with a view to centralization of authority in the crown, further weakening of tribal ties, and attachment of the priesthood to his person. In pursuance of the policy of centralization, the tribal divisions were replaced for administrative purposes by twelve roughly similar prefectures, sometimes more or less co-terminous with the old tribes, but more often diverging sharply from them. The new prefects, whose names are listed in I Kings 4, seem to have been officials from the royal entourage; two of them are stated to have married daughters of Solomon—a clear illustration of the methods employed to secure their loyalty to the crown. It has been urged that Judah was excluded from the number of prefectures and that it enjoyed preferential treatment, but I Kings 4:19-20 seems to contradict this interpretation, which disagrees strikingly with the efforts of David to place the crown above tribal divisions.[119] A principal duty of these prefects was to furnish provisions for the royal court, each for a month. If the daily amount recorded in I Kings 5:2 ff. is correct, the average quantity of provision supplied by each prefecture in a year was something like 900 *kor* of semolina, 1,800 of wheat flour, 900 oxen, 3,000 sheep, etc.[120] Since the *kor* was roughly equivalent to six bushels, this was a very heavy drain on a population which probably averaged less than 100,000 for each prefecture, including Canaanites. Small wonder that Israel rebelled after Solomon's death!

The seventy years during which David and Solomon ruled a united Israel were a time of extraordinary material and cultural progress. A great many new towns and villages were built all over the country, and the population may easily have doubled, from a possible 400,000 to a possible 800,000 (counting only Israelites). Public security was so improved that the large subterranean grain pits which were so characteristic of the preceding age vanish from the excavated sites of the time. Architecture, art and music developed amazingly. The increased popularity of literature may be gauged by David's own reputation as a psalmist, and especially by Solomon's even greater fame as poet and author of proverbs and fables. It may be doubted whether Solomon's literary craftsmanship was sufficiently appealing to subsequent generations to have survived intact, as some of David's compositions unquestionably did; but who can say how much of it may not be embedded in the post-exilic anthologies of Proverbs and Canticles? In any event, it is certain that classical Hebrew prose attained definite form and canons during Solomon's reign, as vividly illustrated by the beautifully written narrative of the events preceding and accompanying the death of David and Solomon's own accession to the throne. From the forms of Egyptian names and other hints, it has frequently been surmised that such sections of the JE[121] narratives of Genesis as the story of Joseph took their present literary form at that time. However this may be, the age was certainly characterized by a flowering of literature. Some day we may have archaeological documentation of the increasing use of the art of writing at that time; at present we have only one Hebrew inscription which can be attributed with confidence to the reign of Solomon or immediately afterwards—the Gezer Calendar, a school exercise containing a mnemonic ditty listing the periods of the agricultural year.[122] To the schoolboy in question and to his teacher we owe a debt of gratitude, since this priceless little document furnishes us invaluable data for the history of Hebrew script and spelling. Such objective contemporary data are worth far more for the critical student of the Hebrew biblical text than any amount of deduction from subjectively constructed premises.

VI FROM THE DISRUPTION OF THE MONARCHY TO THE REVOLT OF JEHU

Solomon's cavalier disregard of time-honored tribal and individual rights was bound to alienate an increasing number of his subjects, especially in the northern part of the country, where blood ties and rewards of empire were much less effective than in the south. Hardly had Solomon died, *c.* 922 B.C.,[123] when rebellion flared up against his son, Rehoboam. The revolt was headed by Jeroboam, an Ephraimite from Zeredah, southwest of Shechem.[124] Jeroboam had been an official in charge of the Josephite corvée employed by Solomon in fortifying Jerusalem, but was forced to flee to the protection of Shishak, king of Egypt. The latter, a powerful Libyan noble, had dethroned Psusennes II, last of the Tanite house (*c.* 935 B.C.), and had made himself king in his place, founding the Bubastite (Twenty-second) Dynasty.[125] Shishak replaced the weak, quasi-priestly rule of the Tanites by a dynamic policy of aggression, illustrated by his protection of the Edomite, Hadad, and the North Israelite, Jeroboam, against their suzerain in Jerusalem. If Rehoboam had been able to strike at once against the still unorganized North Israelites, he might have won; that the attack was not launched must probably be credited in large part to a warning from Shishak, who was doubtless already plotting to disrupt the Solomonic empire. At all events, Rehoboam was sufficiently alarmed by the threat of Egyptian invasion to abandon any projected punitive expedition and to fortify a large number of strategically located points commanding roads and valleys leading into Judah from the south and west. Fifteen of these fortified towns are listed by the Chronicler; they were admirably selected to create the strongest practicable defense line against attack by an Egyptian army.[126] When the invasion finally came, in the fifth year of Rehoboam (c. 918 B.C.), it broke with tremendous force over Judah and its Philistine and Edomite dependencies. In the great Karnak List Shishak listed over 150 places which he claimed to have taken; the presence of many Edomite names in this list has only recently been recognized.[127] Archaeological evidence confirms the accounts in Kings and Chronicles: the huge Egyptian host, consisting largely of barbarian contingents from Libya and Ethiopia, carried fire and sword over the country, utterly devastating such towns as Debir and probably Beth-shemesh. Once in Asia, Shishak proceeded to lay Israel as well as Judah waste; the correctness of the inclusion of North Israelite towns in the list has been demonstrated by the discovery of a fragment of a large triumphal stele of Shishak at Megiddo, one of the towns listed at Karnak as conquered. Having unleashed the Egyptian terror on Judah, Jeroboam was to have much the same experience as Stalin nearly three thousand years later, when the Nazis turned against Russia after conquering Poland.

Meanwhile Jeroboam proceeded with no little shrewdness to break the links connecting the northern tribes to Jerusalem. There is reason to think that he kept the administrative structure as intact as was practicable; it can scarcely be accidental that the provincial organization of North Israel in the eighth century was still modeled after the administrative reorganization of Solomon, with western Manasseh, Gilead, Dor and Megiddo forming independent prefectures.[128] Even his strangely archaic name, which probably means "May the People Multiply," is obviously modeled after the equally archaic name of his rival, Rehoboam (for Yirhab 'am, "May the People Expand"). It must be remembered that throne names were by no means restricted to Egypt; we know six or seven dual names of kings of Judah, beginning with Solomon (Jedidiah), and at least two of kings of Aram. It is quite possible that Jeroboam selected Shechem as his first capital at least partly because it lay outside the strictly Israelite tribal system, being an older Canaanite-Hebrew enclave in Manasseh.[129] In moving from Shechem to Tirzah, he may also have selected an old Canaanite town which was not even yet considered as strictly within the tribal system. In his religious reorganization Jeroboam had to go back to earlier precedents than those of the Davidides, since they had done their work of attaching the Elide family and the traditional system of worship to Jerusalem surpassingly well. Probably to old North Israelite practice went back the tradition portraying the invisible presence of Yahweh as standing on the back of a young bull—certainly the same young bull on which the ancient storm-god of southwestern Asia was represented as standing (usually visible, sometimes invisible) from the third millennium B.C. to the fourth century A.D.[130] According to the JE tradition of Ex. 32, the golden bull-calf had already been introduced into Israelite cult by Aaron himself, during the lifetime of Moses. Conceptually this practice was no more idolatrous than the equally symbolic representation of Yahweh in the Temple of Solomon as an invisible Presence enthroned on the cherubim.[131] In practice, however, the pagan associations of the young bull were likely to lead to paganizing theology and to encouragement of syncretism. The latter undoubtedly took place; we have no direct evidence for the former, and the name 'Egel-yau, borne by an Israelite of the mid-eighth century whose name occurs in the Ostraca of Samaria, meant merely "Young Bull of Yahweh," expressing full recognition of the fact that the bulls were not themselves gods, but were merely ministers of Deity. As sites for the chief centers of the reorganized Yahweh cult Jeroboam selected Bethel and Dan, both because of their strategic locations and because of their significance as ancient pilgrimage shrines. The priesthood of Dan claimed descent from Moses, that of Bethel probably from Aaron—a claim explicitly rejected by the priests of Jerusalem.

Meanwhile the paganizing tendencies initiated in Jerusalem by Solomon himself, both through the complex ritual and elaborate decoration of the Temple (which now included a much greater measure of Canaanite elements than ever before) and through his uxorious toleration of foreign cults across the Kedron Valley from the Temple, were bearing fruit. Rehoboam's second successor, Asa, was only a child at the death of his brother, Abijah, and he remained for fourteen years under the regency of the queen mother, Maachah. Rehoboam's mother had been an Ammonite princess, and Maachah belonged to the family of the half-pagan Absalom, so paganism was ascendant on the distaff side. Small wonder that Maachah was an open worshiper of Asherah, the great Canaanite goddess of fertility! Fortunately the young king sided with the Yahwists, and when he became old enough to take power into his own hands, he inaugurated a drastic reformation, restoring monotheism to its old place of honor in Judah.[132] In judging the frequent triumphs of Canaanite polytheism in Israel, we must always bear in mind that polytheism had a popular appeal in many ways like that of the dominant secularism of our own day. The wealth, science and aesthetic culture of that age were lined up on the side of Canaanite religion, thanks to the unprecedented progress made by the great Phoenician cities and their smaller counterparts on the coastal plain of Palestine. Compared with Phoenicia, the lands of Judah and Israel were very poor, very rustic and far behind the spirit of the day in fashions, arts of civilization and material pleasures of life. All the sinister fascination of the elaborate proto-sciences of magic and divination was marshaled in defense of polytheism against the stern, almost savage, simplicity of Mosaic theology. When Israelite women employed the same amulets as their Canaanite friends in order to ward off evil spirits, they unconsciously made it more difficult to save their children from the perils of the Canaanite way of life. The extraordinary thing is that the way of Moses succeeded in Israel in spite of the forces drawn up against it!

Meanwhile the intermittent struggle between Judah and Israel continued. Abijah is credited with having won an important victory over Jeroboam. However, Israel's potential power was so much greater than Judah's, especially after the devastation of the latter by Shishak, that such victories had no more than ephemeral significance. Moreover, Asa had to repel at least one invasion from the direction of Egypt, probably carried out by an Ethiopian garrison commander from the Egyptian frontier fortress of Gerar. Whether Zerah "the Ethiopian" was acting on orders from Shishak's successor, Osorkon I, we are not told, but it seems likely enough. But when Baasha of Israel undertook hostile acts on the northern frontier, Asa sent envoys to Ben-Hadad of Aram, whom he readily persuaded to invade Israel from the north. The resulting invasion (*c.* 878 B.C.) devastated northern Galilee, and probably led—directly or indirectly—to the loss of all Israelite territory east of the Jordan and north of the Yarmuk. Thus Asa brought the downfall of all Israel a step nearer. Stern as the lesson was, it seems to have been learned, and relations between the two Israelite states remained, in general, friendly for the following century and a half.

Under the long reigns of Asa (*c.* 913-873 B.C.) and Jehoshaphat (*c.* 873-849 B.C.) the house of David was solidly established on the throne of Judah. Since they controlled Edom, as far as the Gulf of 'Aqabah, these kings were able to hold exclusive control over the caravan trade from Arabia, except in so far as the caravans stopped at Midianite ports farther south. The traditions concerning their wealth are probably true in substance. Monotheistic circles remembered them, particularly Jehoshaphat, for their support of Yahweh against pagan deities and practices. In Jehoshaphat's reign, according to the Chronicler, there was an exceedingly important administrative change—the replacement, by royally appointed judges, of the older administration of customary law by local elders, and the establishment of a court of appeals in Jerusalem, formed of religious and tribal heads.[133] From this time on it became necessary to codify civil legislation, in order to furnish the directives without which no royal judiciary could long maintain the respect of the people.

In North Israel, on the other hand, the stability of the crown became steadily less, if possible. Jeroboam's son Nadab was assassinated in the second year of his reign and was replaced by Baasha, to whom his murder was attributed. Baasha's son, Elah, was in his turn, according to our tradition, assassinated by Zimri in the second year of his reign—a remarkable example of poetic justice. Zimri massacred all male members of the house of Baasha, but was himself burned to death in his palace by Omri; the latter was forced to fight for some time with a certain Tibni before he could become sole ruler of northern Israel (*c.* 876 B.C.). By this time Israel had lost eastern Palestine north of the Yarmuk to Aram (see above), and the region just north of the Arnon had been occu-

pied by the resurgent Moabites. It is sometimes inferred from
the rapid change of rulers in North Israel during the first half
century after the Disruption that its monarchy was elective.
This idea is extremely improbable: it is quite enough to
recognize that the idea of charismatic leadership was still very
much alive, and that there was no combination of extraordinary qualities of leadership and religious sanction in North
Israel to assure the permanence of a dynasty there.

Omri's prestige and qualities of leadership were such that
he was able to hand the throne down to his grandsons. During
the decades of the Omride Dynasty (c. 876-842 B.C.) Israel
was consolidated and saved from further disintegration.
Thanks to the Mesha Stele, we know that Omri reconquered
Moab and resettled Israelites in the territory north of the
Arnon; he also seems to have been victorious against Aram.
At the same time, Omri oriented his policy westward, toward
the Mediterranean and Phoenicia. About 870 B.C. he transferred his capital from Tirzah, which faced eastward, to the
splendid new site of Samaria, facing westward toward the
Mediterranean and northwestward toward Phoenicia. Crowfoot's excavations have proved that Reisner was wrong in dif-
ferentiating between a building period of Omri and a second
of Ahab; actually Omri can only have begun construction of
the city, which was continued by his son Ahab without interruption.[134] Omri's friendly relationship to Phoenicia was sealed
by marriage of his crown prince to Jezebel, daughter of Itto-
baal, the Sidonian king of Tyre (887-856 B.C.). One important reason for this alliance was undoubtedly the common
danger to both constituted by the steady expansion of the
power of Ben-Hadad, king of Aram (c. 880-842 B.C.). The
alliance proved fatal to the permanence of the dynasty, but it
probably brought considerable wealth to both Omri and Ahab
through the accompanying expansion of trade relations between Israel and Phoenicia. By this time North Africa and
Spain, as well as Sardinia, had certainly been colonized, and
Sidonian power was at its height.

Ahab, however, had to fight several wars against Aram,
mainly defensive. Owing to lack of contemporary records it is
quite impossible to reconstruct the complex interplay of politi-

cal forces.[135] It is very important, however, to note that the threat of Assyrian expansion had again become real after the North Syrian campaign of Asshur-nasir-apli about 870 B.C., which followed more than a century during which there is no trace of Assyrian activity west of the Euphrates. It was not, however, until 853 that the next Assyrian king, Shalmaneser III, felt himself strong enough to make a direct attack on the powerful Syrian states of Hamath and Aram. Ben-Hadad (called Hadad-ezer, evidently his personal name, by the Assyrians) had learned of the projected invasion a long time in advance, thanks probably to the use of such telegraphic devices as fire signaling, with which the inscriptions of Mari and Lachish have made us familiar. Marshaling his forces, which included well-organized armies provided by the three main allies, the kings of Hamath, Aram and Israel, as well as small contingents from many other more insignificant sources, the Aramean met the Assyrian at Qarqar in the territory of Hamath. The battle appears to have been indecisive; at all events the Assyrians were forced to withdraw and it was not until 848 that they resumed the war against the Syrian confederates. In the interim, war between Aram and Israel broke out again, resulting in the death of Ahab before Ramoth-gilead on the northeastern frontier, the site of which has been found by Nelson Glueck. The most interesting point about this battle is that Jehoshaphat of Judah was Ahab's ally against Aram, thus beginning a defensive alliance which seems to have lasted until the downfall of the Omride house.

Ahab and Jezebel will be remembered to the end of recorded history, not because of their own little personalities, but because of the towering figure of the dour Gileadite, whom they despised but also feared, and whose influence was to bring their house to ruin. We know little about the man, Elijah, but more about his great deeds, and much more about the tremendous influence which he exerted on his own and all subsequent ages. Elijah came after the prophets of Yahweh had been recognized as a special class or body of inspired preachers and reformers for over a century and a half. The example of the great Samuel, who rebuked Saul, had been followed by Nathan, David's mentor, and Gad; by Ahijah the Shilonite,

critic of Jeroboam, and Jehu ben Hanani, who attacked
Baasha; and in Judah by Shemaiah and Azariah, little though
we may know about them. Elijah stood in the direct line of
this tradition. The prophet of Yahweh was still an inspired
seer, whose oracles followed the ecstatic model and were seldom
remembered long; the time had not come for marvelous poetic
sermons, composed in advance, delivered orally and written
down later by enthralled listeners or recited from generation to
generation until collected into anthologies by later scholars.
Pious Israelites were not far wrong in distinguishing between
true prophets and false prophets of Yahweh by the impact of
their words on the privileged classes; if the latter were pleased
the prophet was false; if they were displeased the prophet was
true.

The traditions regarding Elijah are few in number but rich
in content; they paint their subject in unforgettable strokes.
Elijah is described as a displaced person (*toshab*) from Gilead,
who was thus without property. A man of wild places and
deserts, he went for refreshment to the Mountain of God,
where Moses had once brought Israel to the feet of Yahweh.
To him Jerusalem and Bethel were perhaps equally objection-
able from the standpoint of authentic Mosaic tradition, but
tradition recalled only his vastly greater wrath at the abominations of Baal, honored in Israel as never before. The princess
of Tyre had brought with her the cult of the great Tyrian
divinities, Baal-Melcarth and Asherah. It was not only to
Israel that Melcarth gained access with Jezebel; a recently
published stele of Ben-Hadad of Aram, dating about 850 B.C.,
contains a votive dedication to Melcarth, whose cult may possibly have been popularized in Aram by another Tyrian
princess.[136] Asherah's special connection with Tyre is already
attested by the Keret Epic, five hundred years before Jezebel.[137]
Against the profligate abandon of the cult of Melcarth and
Asherah Elijah reacted with merciless severity. Not for him
were the civilized reactions of an Ahab; he stood in the tradition of Samuel, to whom wholesale *herem* (sacrificial destruction) was the only way to suppress the abominations of
Canaanite civilization. To Elijah, justice to the poor and the
widow was paramount; in those years of increasing wealth and

luxury too many Israelites were forgetting the apodictic law of Moses: "Thou shalt not . . ." Not long after the prophet's death the dynasty of Omri collapsed amid torrents of blood, the inevitable end of an evil period. But for Elijah we should probably know virtually nothing of it but the names and regnal years of its kings.

FROM JEHU TO
THE FALL OF SAMARIA
VII

No revolution is described in the Bible with such wealth of
detail as Jehu's rebellion against the house of Omri. Several
aspects of the revolution appear clearly. In the first place, it
was a religious upheaval, in which the fiery propaganda of
Elijah and his successor, Elisha, briefly reached its goal, that
of extirpating the cult of Baal-Melcarth from Israelite soil.
In the course of the ensuing blood purge, not only were all the
Omrides and their more prominent supporters liquidated,
there was also a wholesale slaughter of all captured priests,
prophets and votaries of Baal. Closely linked with the religious
upheaval was a socio-economic revolution, in which the poor
and the landless revolted against the increasing contrast between the wealth of the new nobility and the equally new merchant class, on the one hand, and the poverty of the masses, on
the other. The years of famine which dogged the Omride period had compelled the peasants to mortgage their lands and
sell their children in order to eke out a bare subsistence. As a
result of the symbiotic trading relationship set up by Solomon
and later by Omri with Phoenicia, wealth had undoubtedly
poured into Israel, as vividly illustrated by the excavations at
Samaria. When hard times came to the peasants, the wealthy
merchants lent them the necessary funds to tide them over—
at usurious rates of interest, just as has been the practice in
Palestine and Syria since time immemorial. In this unpre-
dictable Mediterranean climate periods of rainy years alternate
irregularly with periods of dry years, carrying with them
constant movement of men and money, and dooming the
peasantry to periodic ruin unless protected by enlightened government policy. But no famine was as long remembered as the
great drought of Ahab's time, recorded also in Tyrian annals.

The episode of Naboth, a particularly bad perversion of justice, became the dominant theme in the upsurge of popular discontent. Extremists like the Rechabites, who rejected agriculture and the amenities as well as the vices of sedentary society, joined Jehu; tradition credits the Rechabite leader, Jonadab, with an active part in the bloodiest phase of the revolution. A third aspect of the revolution was military: the army officers, led by Jehu, were dissatisfied with the weak policy of the crown, which they presumably associated with the luxurious indolence of the privileged classes and the dominance of Phoenician religion and culture.

Had Jehu been himself a great man, he might have reunited Israel and deferred the day of reckoning. Unfortunately, there is nothing in his record to suggest ability, and the situation of the Northern Kingdom declined rapidly under Jehu and his son, Joahaz. By the sanguinary thoroughness of his blood purge he had irremediably antagonized Israel's previous friends, Judah and Phoenicia. Judah's king and king's brothers had been butchered, while the deaths among Phoenicians, from Jezebel down, were extremely numerous, and the insult to Melcarth, lord of Tyre, was irrevocable in character. Deprived of help from these former allies, Israel's situation became rapidly desperate. Hazael of Aram overran and apparently annexed the whole of Israelite Trans-Jordan. In 841 Jehu docilely paid tribute to the king of Assyria, in connection with Shalmaneser's attack on Hazael, in which the Arameans suffered severely but did not capitulate. But no more help came from Assyria. After 837 B.C., when the Assyrians raided the northeastern end of Hazael's territory, the kingdom of Aram was not molested again until 805, shortly after the death of Hazael. Assyria had its own problems: for six years there was civil war, followed by a painful process of consolidation for eleven years, and then by the regency of Semiramis for four additional years.[138] Under Jehu's son Joahaz (c. 815-801 B.C.) Israel was devastated by the Arameans and reduced to a dependency of Aram. The king was allowed a bodyguard of only ten chariots and fifty horsemen—in contrast to Ahab's reported two thousand chariots at Qarqar. The chariot cities founded by Solomon were left empty, in particular Megiddo, which was destroyed and does not seem to have been rebuilt immediately. Hazael carried his arms southward on both sides of the Jordan, overrunning Philistia and levying a calamitous tribute on Judah.

Meanwhile Judah had also had a revolution, though a much milder affair. Ahab's sister or daughter, Athaliah, had been married to Jehoshaphat's son, Jehoram. After the latter's son, Ahaziah, was killed by Jehu in 842, the queen mother seized power, killing all the Davidides who appeared to threaten her status. She was also a votary of Baal, whose high priest, Mattan, bore a typically Phoenician name, suggesting that the god in question was the same Tyrian Melcarth whose cult had already been diffused in Israel and Aram. Fortunately Jehoash, one of Ahaziah's sons, had been saved by his aunt, who was wife of Jehoiada, high priest of Yahweh. When revolt finally broke out about 837 B.C. the young prince was set on the throne. Athaliah and Mattan were killed, but nothing is said of any further blood purge, suggesting that there was little of the intense socio-economic feeling in Judah that had led to such excesses a few years earlier in Israel. The reign of Jehoash (c. 837-800 B.C.) was in no sense brilliant; his crushing humiliation at the hands of Hazael of Aram has been mentioned. Nor was the reign of his son, Amaziah, much more remarkable; he reconquered Edom, which had rebelled successfully against Judah half a century before, but was disastrously defeated by Joash, king of Israel. It is characteristic that both Jehoash and Amaziah were assassinated in palace revolts, and that tradition remembered both of them in terms which mix praise with blame almost equally.

The turn of Israel's fortunes was not long in coming. In 805 the young Assyrian king, Adad-nirari III, resumed aggressive policy in Syria, and by 802 Aram was prostrate; its king is said to have paid no less than a hundred talents of gold and a thousand of silver to the triumphant Assyrians. About 801 Joash became king of Israel, and in the ensuing war with Ben-Hadad, Hazael's son, he recovered the territory previously lost to Aram. By the time of his death he had also reduced Judah to a vassal state, setting the stage for the brilliant reign of his son, Jeroboam II (c. 786-746 B.C.). Under the latter the

Northern Kingdom reached the summit of its material power and wealth, expanding northward at the expense of Damascus and Hamath, and southward—as would appear from a defective text, II Kings 14:28—at the expense of Judah. Archaeology contributes further details, illustrating the development of architecture at Samaria and Megiddo, as well as the flowering of the arts. During this entire period Assyria was weak, scarcely able to maintain her foothold in Syria by repeated campaigns against Hamath and Damascus. Moreover, Hamath and Damascus were themselves engaged in a bitter conflict for supremacy in Syria, vividly described in the contemporary stele of Zakir, king of Hamath. At that time Phoenician colonial expansion was at its height, and wealth poured into the treasuries of its great cities. Greek competition was actively beginning, and in less than a century the Greeks and the Assyrians were to deal terrific blows against the merchant princes of Tyre and Sidon. But Phoenicia was still a neighbor from which Israel could gain immense riches, both through the sale of Israelite products to the overcrowded Phoenician seacoast and through direct investment of capital and manpower in Phoenician enterprises. Tolls on caravans passing through Israel from Arabia were presumably also an important source of revenue.

The wealth and power of Israel under Jeroboam II meant great material progress and a notable rise in the standard of living; they also brought with them again increasing disparity between the lot of the rich and that of the poor, and increasing moral corruption, further augmented by the infiltration of inherited Canaanite customs and new Mediterranean practices into Israel over the long common border with Phoenicia. Moreover, the disastrous rout of Melcarth and his followers had by no means eradicated the older cult of Baal, especially in the old Canaanite towns which lined the plains. According to II Kings 13:6 Jehu and his son did not remove the Asherah from Samaria; we may perhaps surmise that this Asherah had existed before the importation of the cult of the Tyrian Melcarth and Asherah, and was considered as less obnoxious. However this may be, the personal names on the Ostraca from Samaria, dating from 738-736 (Yigael Yadin), show that names formed with "Baal" were still roughly in the ratio of 7:11 to names formed with "Yahweh." Allowing for a certain preponderance in favor of the latter among abbreviated names, we should still have fully half as many Baal names as Yahweh names. Since we can no longer reckon with the possibility that Baal was a recognized appellation of the God of Israel, it follows that Baalism was still the basic religion of a large proportion of the people of the land. The contemporary situation in Judah was very different; Baal names—which had been fairly common in the tenth century—never appear in our literary or epigraphic sources of the eighth and seventh centuries B.C.

This is the background against which we must set the poetic sermons of Amos and Hosea. If Morgenstern's plausible combination is correct,[139] we may date the beginning of Amos's prophetic career about 752; his last datable prophecy was delivered not long after 738 B.C. Hosea's poetic sermons seem to extend from before 746 to after 735. Both are fine examples of the true prophet of Yahweh, who felt it as his primary function to rebuke his people and rulers for breaking the law of Yahweh. In their public appearances we see scarcely a trace of the old ecstatic; in their poetic addresses there is careful preparation, but along original lines, drawing little from older poetic literature, perhaps because of the strong Canaanite element embedded in the latter. In both these prophets we find constant awareness of the JE tradition of Israel's beginnings and the Mosaic period; both show their point of view by stressing the divine *Torah*. In these prophets we do not have innovators, but reformers like Samuel and Elijah, reformers who reflect a gentler, more refined age, in which love had become more potent than hate and a cosmopolitan spirit looked at Israel and Judah almost as impartially as it considered their neighbors. It is not their zeal for monotheism, but rather their more advanced culture and their sensitivity to more refined spiritual nuances that set Amos and Hosea apart from their precursors in Israel. Hosea inveighs against all forms of religious practice which diverge from the strict tradition of Mosaic monotheism, whether the cult of Baal, the cults of the high places, or the cults of Yahweh at Bethel and Dan. Both prophets are horrified by the selfish luxury, the immorality and the oppression of the poor that they see around them, but neither of them ever makes the modern mistake of distinguishing sharply between individual morality and social welfare. In that relatively simple age it was clear enough that each entailed the other; neither was possible alone.

Under the long reign of Uzziah (Azariah), *c.* 783-742 B.C., Judah reached the summit of its power. The fame of Uzziah's reign was second only to that of Solomon in succeeding generations, as we know from the Chronicler and from such testimonies as the Herodian plaque honoring the last resting place of the king's reputed bones, discovered by E. L. Sukenik.[140] Ascending the throne as a lad of sixteen, several years after the accession of Jeroboam II, it does not seem likely that Uzziah reached the summit of his power until after the sun of Jeroboam had begun to set. Meanwhile Uzziah was busily engaged in building up economic and military strength. The Chronicler's description of his efforts to develop the economic resources of the country is most instructive, and is confirmed by archaeological indications, which prove that the most active period of construction in the Negeb was precisely in the eighth century B.C. The penetration of Jewish enterprise into Arabia at the time is attested by the discovery of a seal of Jotham, Uzziah's son and regent, in Nelson Glueck's excavations at Ezion-geber; that the king built Eloth near Ezion-geber is stated in II Chron. 26:2.[141] Uzziah's military program is also described in some detail by the Chronicler, who credits him with the introduction of siege engines into Judah. Uzziah appears to have conquered the northern and eastern part of the Philistine plain, thus controlling the important caravan routes in the Coastal Plain. The Chronicler lays great stress on his military activities in Arabia (still clearer in the Greek version), which were evidently designed to consolidate his position on the caravan routes from Arabia. About 750 Uzziah was stricken with leprosy and his place in public was taken by his son, Jotham, officially designated as regent. However, Uzziah seems still to have been the real ruler, and when Tiglath-pileser III of Assyria invaded Syria in 743 and the immediately following years, he credits him (under the alternative name Azariah) with being the head of the anti-Assyrian party in the west.[142] This assertion is in every way reasonable. Jeroboam II, who had been the strongest ruler in the west, died about 746 and was replaced for six months by his son, Zechariah. The latter was killed in a revolt, which placed a certain Shallum on the throne for a month, after which Menahem seized the throne, following a civil war remembered for Menahem's atrocities. During this period Judah was the most stable state in Palestine and probably in all Syria, where inscriptions indicate a more or less continuous state of internecine war. Judah's wealth and military establishment were thus calculated to place her in the forefront of any plan for a coalition against the resurgent power of Assyria.

However, it was too late. Jotham was replaced by his son, Ahaz, about 735, and Ahaz found himself at once the target of an attack by Menahem's second successor, Pekah, and the latter's ally, Rezin, king of Aram.[143] Ahaz appealed to Assyria for help, which was promptly forthcoming; Damascus was stormed by the Assyrians in 732, after a bloody war, and Aram was converted into four Assyrian provinces. Even before the fall of Damascus the Assyrian armies swept over Israel, devastating Galilee, and annexing all of Israel except Ephraim and western Manasseh (733 B.C.). In 732 the Assyrians appointed Hoshea as the last king of Samaria, but the Assyrian exactions were too much for him, and he rebelled about 724, relying on the very dubious promise of Egyptian assistance. Egypt was then broken up into many small city-states, and the "king" in question, Siwe, or possibly Sibe, appears outside of the Bible and the Assyrian inscriptions only doubtfully on a single scarab![144] Hoshea was immediately taken prisoner, but the capital held out against a besieging army for over two years, falling late in the year 722/1. Hebrew tradition attributed its capture to Shalmaneser V (727-722), but in his inscriptions Sargon II (722-705) repeatedly boasts of his conquest of Samaria and the "wide land of Beth-Omri" (official Israelite name of Samaria).[145] Hebrew tradition is probably right, but Sargon may well have seized power in Assyria before the actual fall of the city. He claims to have taken 27,290 Israelites into captivity.

This does not, of course, mean for a moment that the

northern tribes of Israel vanished from the historical scene, never to reappear except possibly in some remote land to which they had wandered. We now know that the Israelites continued to occupy most of Ephraim and parts of Galilee and Gilead, and that there were Israelite minorities in Ammon, Syria and Phoenicia. In seventh-century Mesopotamia we find Israelites established in the region of Gozan as well as in Assyria proper.[146] The book of Tobit confirms the information to be gleaned from the Bible and the Assyrian inscriptions about the settlement in Media of deportees from Northern Israel. At a time when Tobit was thought to date from not earlier than the second century B.C., its testimony had little value, but we now know that the original language of the book was Imperial Aramaic and that it must date from the fourth or even the fifth century B.C.[147] The influence of the northern diaspora, which may have been larger numerically than the southern, on the evolution of Judaism cannot be ignored. Eventually all Yahwists came to be known as Jews, but in Ezekiel we find "Israel" almost invariably preferred as a designation to "Judah," and the Essenes of the second century B.C. deliberately chose to be called "Israelites" rather than "Jews." In the writer's opinion, the Books of Job and Jonah were North Israelite, probably composed in Phoenicia or Syria in the seventh century B.C.[148]

JUDAH FROM THE FALL OF SAMARIA TO THE CAPTIVITY

VIII

It was now a century and a half since the Assyrians had resumed their remorseless march of empire. It was only a quarter of a century since a revitalized Assyria had begun to crush the kingdoms of Arpad and Hamath. Every few years since then brought with it the end of some once strong native state. In 732 Damascus had fallen and the glory of Aram was but a memory; in 721 Samaria followed her long-time rival. . . . Such considerations must have made every man of Judah tremble for the future of his little state, the last barrier between Assyria and the caravan routes of the South. In the new age no man was secure, and no city could hope for prolonged existence. Ahaz had indeed surrendered to his powerful ally in the war against Aram and Israel, but there is no reason to suppose that Judah's burden of taxation was at all reduced because of her favored status. However, Ahaz had saved his country from devastation, and archaeological indications point to increasing prosperity toward the end of the eighth century B.C. Uzziah had laid sound foundations for economic development. Moreover, it appears that the increasing prosperity of Judah was not channeled for the exclusive benefit of the aristocracy and the wealthy merchants, as was apparently true of the Northern Kingdom in the eighth century (see above). The excavations at Debir show that there was an extraordinary homogeneity of population there between 750 and 589 B.C., at least if we may judge from the fact that all private houses so far excavated reflect a surprisingly narrow range of variation in social scale. The citizens of the town seem to have been almost exclusively engaged in one type of industry, to the exclusion of all others aside from normal rural pursuits: the weaving and dyeing of woolen goods.[149] Explicit biblical statements, referring to the late pre-exilic age, show that there were other such concentrations of craftsmen in Judah, notably of potters, linenworkers, metalworkers, while in Jerusalem there were quarters devoted to bakers and goldsmiths.[150] Significantly enough, these references appear mostly in connection with genealogical lists, indicating clearly that there was a relatively direct passage from the old clan system to a new guild system. In other words, there was no period in Judah during which there was such concentration of wealth in the hands of individuals (aside from the crown) as to destroy the old social order, a fact which explains in part why there is no such bitter denunciation of the dominant social order in Isaiah or Micah as we find in Hosea. It is more than likely that some enlightened person or movement was at least partly responsible for the development of the guild system in Judah, perhaps on Phoenician models; but its growth in a semi-patriarchal society would have been unthinkable if Judah had not lagged considerably behind Israel in the evolution of ancestral Hebrew institutions, at the same time that it enjoyed nearly the same opportunities for commercial and industrial expansion.

The stage was thus set for both religious reform and political activism. On the one hand, the people found themselves faced by rapidly approaching doom, borne by swift horsemen from the north. Against the overwhelming might of Asshur only Yahweh could stand; without Him His followers were helpless. On the other hand, new prosperity and new economic opportunities made men increasingly restive under the grinding taxation necessary to meet rapacious Assyrian demands for tribute and irregular levies of every kind. So when Ahaz died, some six years after the Fall of Samaria,[151] and was replaced by an energetic young prince, Hezekiah, there was a rapid change in both religious and political policy.

Owing to unwarranted depreciation of the data preserved for us by the Chronicler, most recent historians have failed fully to understand the religious situation under Hezekiah. By the latter's accession devout Yahwistic circles in Judah had progressed in their iconoclasm far beyond the policy of tolerating traditional Israelite religious practices and semi-pagan cultic institutions which had characterized the official atti-

tude of the earlier Divided Monarchy. Moreover, the cata-
strophic collapse of Samaria, effectively utilized by the Prophets,
strongly reinforced the reform party. Hezekiah proceeded, accordingly, to eliminate the high places and to destroy the
altars, standing stones (*massebot*) and related objects, associated by the masses with local cults of Yahweh; he even went
so far as to destroy no less sacred an object than the copper
representation of a snake which had been preserved in the
Temple, and which was reputed to have been made by Moses.
That this reform was only partly successful need not surprise
us; such iconoclastic efforts on the part of a minority to change
time-honored customs require wholehearted acceptance by the
masses before they are likely to succeed.

At the same time Hezekiah and his supporters began active
missionary propaganda in Northern Israel; the Chronicler tells
us that it met with some success in Galilee but was unfavorably
received in Ephraim. This is not surprising, since the rival
sanctuary of Bethel had been reorganized under Assyrian provincial auspices in order to compete with Jerusalem for the
religious support of the people of Ephraim (II Kings 17:27-
28). We may safely assume that the political aspects of this
missionary propaganda were not lost on the Assyrian governors
of Samaria, who were having difficulty keeping the Israelite
population subjugated, as we learn from Assyrian sources.

While Sargon II of Assyria was alive, Judah apparently did
not go beyond planning for future revolt. The Assyrian inscriptions inform us that the king of Ashdod, then the most important Philistine city, tried to obtain the aid of Judah in his
projected rebellion. However this may be, the Assyrian com-
mander-in-chief (Isa. 20:1) attacked Ashdod, reduced it and
made it an Assyrian province in 711 B.C. Egyptian support,
which had also been sought by the rebels of Ashdod, failed
notably, eliciting bitter taunts from both Isaiah and the contemporary Assyrian historian. Even if Hezekiah had become
involved in the rebellion, he withdrew in time, saving Judah
from a futile stand against vastly superior power. So matters
remained for about a decade, during which there were far-
reaching changes in the international situation. Sargon had
died and had been replaced by a greatly inferior son, Sen-

nacherib (705). The Ethiopians, who had previously conquered Upper Egypt (c. 720), had extended their power over
the whole of the Nile Valley (c. 715), and an energetic
Ethiopian king, Shabako, had now unified Egypt again after a
long period of anarchy and internal weakness (c. 709).[152] The
Chaldean chieftain, Merodach-baladan, had re-established himself as king of Babylon and was defying Assyrian efforts to
dislodge him. Under the circumstances, it was to be expected
that Judah would try to throw off the onerous Assyrian yoke.
In preparation for the day of decision, Hezekiah accepted the
overtures made by Babylon and Egypt, intervened in Philistine
affairs in order to strengthen the hands of the local rebels, and
fortified Jerusalem, where he excavated the Siloam tunnel
through the solid rock in order to provide the city with water
in time of siege.

In 701 B.C. the Assyrian army invaded Palestine and
crushed the rebellion, after defeating a large Egyptian and
Ethiopian host which had advanced northward to relieve the
beleaguered town of Ekron. The strong frontier fortress of
Lachish was stormed, as vividly pictured in the Assyrian re-
liefs, and the fortified towns—forty-six in number, according
to the Assyrians—fell in rapid succession. Hezekiah thereupon
capitulated, paying an extremely heavy tribute, listed in detail
by the Assyrian records, which agree substantially with the
much briefer summary in Kings. According to the Assyrian
annals, Sennacherib also turned over a strip of Jewish territory
in the Shephelah to the three neighboring Philistine princi-
palities. What happened subsequently we do not know, though
it appears that the Jewish towns were recovered not long afterwards. Deuteronomic tradition connects a disastrous pestilence
with an Assyrian invasion which took place after the accession
of the Ethiopian prince Taharqo (Tirhakah) to the Egyptian
throne in 689. Since Hezekiah died in 686, the invasion would
have occurred between 689 and 686. Our Assyrian records
close in 689 and we have no record of military doings in Sennacherib's reign thereafter. In 691, however, the Assyrians
were defeated at Khalule by the Babylonians and Elamites, so
it is entirely reasonable to suppose that Hezekiah then began
planning a new revolt with Ethiopian aid, and that he revolted

after Tirhakah's accession. This time the aged Isaiah supported the king, who was saved by the pestilence and apparently died before the Assyrians were able to put a new army into the field.[153]

The period of the two following Assyrian kings, Esarhaddon (681-669) and Asshurbanapal (669-627 B.C.), represented the climax of Assyrian prestige and wealth, though signs of weakness may be discerned by the historian. Esarhaddon conquered Egypt and his son consolidated his father's conquest; his destruction of Thebes in 663 was long remembered (cf. Nah. 3:8). In 652, however, the Assyrian Empire was shaken to its foundation by a bloody civil war which broke out between Asshurbanapal and his brother and vassal Shamash-shum-ukin, king of Babylon, and lasted until the capture of Babylon in 648. Among the states of Syria and Palestine which joined the rebellion may have been Judah (cf. II Chron. 33:11). The Arab tribes of the Syrian Desert, which had been increasing in numbers and pressing northward for several centuries, took advantage of the situation to inundate the regions east of Antilibanus and Jordan. Edom and Moab are named in the Assyrian inscriptions among the regions devastated, and though a Moabite king captured an Arab chief, whom he sent in chains to Nineveh, there can be no doubt that this catastrophe spelled the end of Moab as a strong autonomous state. A vivid contemporary dirge from about 650 B.C., describing the fate of Moab, has been preserved in both Isaiah (15-16) and Jeremiah (48), with variations showing its popularity.[154]

During this period Judah became infected by the prevailing syncretism, and its king, Manasseh, is said to have restored the local shrines of Yahweh, which Hezekiah had destroyed, and to have returned to official recognition of Baalism as well as to the practice of divination and magic. It may be noted that no other period of cuneiform records has yielded any remotely comparable mass of tablets relating to magic and divination, and that the royal Assyrian letters of the time contain innumerable references to astrology and magic. It was practically impossible for a small vassal state to keep from being flooded with such idolatrous and superstitious practices, which were under royal Assyrian protection.

After the accession of Manasseh's young grandson, Josiah, in 640 B.C. the situation changed abruptly. Josiah is said to have been only eight years old at his accession, and his coming of age coincided roughly with the weakened state of Assyria, caused by rebellion during the last years of Asshur-banapal.[155] In 629 he began a purge which seems to have been considerably more thoroughgoing than that of Hezekiah, including objects of local Yahwist cult as well as pagan idols and installations. It appears that this purge coincided with the removal of effective Assyrian domination, since Josiah was able to extend it into Northern Israel including Galilee as well as Ephraim and Manasseh (II Kings 23:19; II Chron. 34:6-7). In particular he destroyed the cultic installations at Bethel, which had long been in active competition, under Assyrian protection, with the Temple in Jerusalem. This purge was unthinkable unless Josiah also exercised political control of the country, either in defiance of Assyria or, more probably, as nominal vassal of the Assyrians, in somewhat the same way as the contemporary Psammetichus of Egypt. As nominal vassal, controlling the Assyrian provinces of Samaria and Megiddo as well as the tributary state of Judah, Josiah would be free to carry out his reforms; this would also explain why biblical tradition has preserved no hint of military action for the re-conquest of Northern Israel. Albrecht Alt and his pupils have effectively demonstrated the importance of this phase of Israelite history.[156] Ever since Hezekiah's missionary activity in the north, the kings of Judah had kept up close relations with their northern relatives. Amon, Manasseh's short-lived son and successor, was the grandson of a notable from the Galilean town of Jotbah (Assyr. Yatbatu, Greek Jotapata). Josiah's own son, Eliakim, was grandson of another notable from the Galilean town of Rumah, near Jotbah.[157] But Necho's invasion of 609 and Josiah's death in battle with him, defending the Megiddo pass on behalf of the Babylonians (to whom he had by this time shifted his loyalty),[158] put an end to these grandiose dreams of a reunited Israel under a prince of the house of David.

CAPTIVITY AND RESTORATION IX

After Josiah's death Judah became a vassal of Egypt for some
six years. Necho deposed Josiah's son, Jehoahaz, and made his
brother Eliakim king in his place, with the crown name
Jehoiakim. Soon afterwards Nebuchadnezzar, son of Nabopo-
lassar, the Chaldean king of Babylon, defeated the Egyptian
army at Carchemish on the Upper Euphrates (605 B.C.), after
which he was called back to Babylon by the death of his
father.[159] That very autumn he was able to invade Syria again,
and in November-December of the following year he captured
and completely destroyed Ascalon, which had become the focus
of resistance to the Babylonian advance. The situation of
Ascalon is vividly illustrated by an Aramaic letter found in
Egypt, which describes the Babylonian advance as far as Aphek
(Ras el-'Ain in the Plain of Sharon).[160] It is interesting to
note that the fall of the important Philistine seaport is mentioned both by Jeremiah (47:5-7) and by the Greek poet Al-
caeus (in a poem preserved by a fragment discovered in
Egypt).[161]

Whether Judah had already submitted to the Chaldeans or
not we cannot say. The Babylonian Chronicle says nothing
about the following three years (603-600) except that the
Babylonian king went to Syria-Palestine, where he marched
around "triumphantly" (shaltanish), and that the Babylonians
and Egyptians fought an inconclusive battle in November-
December 601. For the year 600/599 we are told only that the
king stayed in his own land reorganizing his army for another
attack on Egypt. The following year (599/598) he set up a
base in Syria for the conquest of the Arabs, whose support may
have seemed necessary for the invasion of Egypt.[162] Since II
Kings 24:1 states that Jehoiakim became a vassal of Nebu-

chadnezzar for three years, after which he revolted, and since the revolt must apparently be placed some time before the fall of Jerusalem in March, 597, it would seem that he submitted to the Chaldeans in the course of the year 603/602 and revolted after the retreat of the Babylonian army from Egypt at the end of the Julian year 601. It is curious that nearly the same account is given by the cuneiform scribe of the punitive expeditions against the Arabs in 599/598 and by the Jewish writer of similar raids against Judah during the period of the revolt. In the following year the Chaldean army invaded Judah in earnest, and Jerusalem fell in March, 597. Meanwhile Jehoiakim died or was assassinated, and his young son, Jehoiachin, went into exile in his place (597 B.C.).[163]

Among the most significant of the undertakings that had been sponsored by Josiah must be reckoned the authoritative collection of the historical traditions of Israel into a new corpus, based on the ancient code found in the Temple (II Kings 22:3 ff.). This code was expanded and edited (it is now known as the Book of Deuteronomy), and was supplemented by a collection of the historical traditions of the Conquest (Joshua) and subsequent periods (Judges, Samuel and Kings), with a running theological commentary which pointed out the close relationship between evildoing and divine retribution.[164] Begun after the finding of an ancient code (which had originally been compiled in Northern Israel and was carried to Jerusalem after the Fall of Samaria) in 622 B.C., this great work may not have been completed until years after Josiah's death in 609; it was then brought up to date and re-edited about 560 B.C. The enthusiasm shown by the Deuteronomist for the work of the prophets and the closeness of his style to that of the prose sections of Jeremiah shows that the two were written in the same period and under similar auspices; the striking similarity between the rhetorical style of the Deuteronomist and Jeremiah and that of the Lachish Letters forms a strong additional argument in favor of dating the work of the former in the last generation before the Fall of Jerusalem.

Informing the work of the Deuteronomist is a pronounced archaistic flavor, arising partly from a desire to seek salvation for the tottering land of Judah by going back to Israel's early history.[165] As a conscious effort to recapture the letter and the spirit of Moses, founder of Israel's institutions, it represents a nostalgic return to the past as the source of all good things. No longer was there facile optimism about Israel's future. As the Northern Kingdom and most of its neighbors had fallen, so would Judah unless it abandoned its evil modern ways and its sophisticated adaptations of foreign culture. Some men of Judah went to extremes; among them were the Rechabites, who went so far as to eschew all agriculture along with other innovations of civilization, attracting favorable comment from Jeremiah himself. Like many more recent utopian primitivists, the Rechabites started from a one-sided reconstruction of antiquity.[166]

Jeremiah's poetic addresses to the people of Judah are couched in singularly beautiful verses, which plastically reproduce his intense hatred of paganism, paganizing ritual and all kinds of cant. In particular he attacks conventional exaltation of the Temple and its sacrificial ritual at the expense of elementary justice and kindness. Under such conditions, in which each new reign and each new deportation meant progressive deterioration of morals, only one conclusion was possible for so direct and forthright a thinker as Jeremiah: just as in the past history of Israel wickedness had invariably been followed by political catastrophe, so would be the case again under the prevailing circumstances. For Jeremiah the only way in which Judah could postpone a similar catastrophe was by patient submission to the will of God as manifested in Chaldean domination.[167] Hence Jeremiah set himself against the self-styled patriots of his people, preferring to be despised as a coward and condemned as a collaborationist. It is instructive to note the extent to which Judahite chauvinism, whipped to a frenzy by the oracles of the prophets whom Jeremiah so roundly denounced (Jer. 23:9-32), went, as illustrated by the Lachish Letters. Toward the end of Zedekiah's reign we find the *sarim* (royal officials and notables) denouncing Jeremiah to the king and demanding that he be executed because of his bad influence on the morale of the people (Jer. 38:4). In Lachish Letter No. 6, a patriotic official writing to the commander of the garrison of Lachish complains bitterly about circular letters sent out by the *sarim*, alleging in identical words that "they weaken the hands" of the people.[168] Yet these were the *sarim* who wished to put Jeremiah to death!

The period 598-587 B.C. was charged with unmixed gloom. Jehoiachin had been accompanied into exile by the leading men of Judah and its best craftsmen. Jeremiah spoke scathingly of the qualities of the regent, Zedekiah, and his followers, whom he called "bad figs" as against the "good figs" which had been taken by the Chaldeans. But Zedekiah and his adherents stubbornly followed the path to ruin by conspiring with Psammetichus II and his son Apries against the Chaldean suzerain. From passages in Jeremiah, vividly illustrated by the Lachish Letters, we learn of the successive fall of the towns of the Negeb and the Shephelah, followed by the last siege of Jerusalem. Excavations at Debir and Lachish show the increasing poverty of the country between the two destructions of these towns in 598 and 587.[169] The population of Judah, which had probably passed 250,000 by the end of the eighth century,[170] can scarcely have been over half that number during this interval. Finally, in July-August, 587,[171] Jerusalem was stormed and most of the remaining notables and craftsmen were sent into Babylonian captivity.

The former mayor of the palace,[172] Gedaliah, was appointed governor of Judah by the Chaldeans, and many Jews who had fled to security before the Chaldean advance returned to the country and accepted his authority. The chiefs of the army in the field, who had hidden in the wilds during the siege, entered into negotiations with Gedaliah, but before any arrangement could be reached a certain ultrapatriotic member of the Davidic family, named Ishmael, treacherously assassinated Gedaliah, killing many of his followers, as well as the Chaldeans stationed at Mizpah. The army chiefs then collected a considerable number of the remaining Jews and fled to Egypt, where they entered into military service and were installed as garrison troops at the northern and southern boundaries. A hundred years after their flight to Egypt we begin to learn something of the fortunes of some of their descendants who were settled by the Saite kings at Elephantine (Yeb) before the Persian invasion in 525 B.C. Even after Gedaliah's assassination, however, there were still enough Jews of rank or skill left in the land to provoke the Chaldeans to a third deportation (582 B.C.).

In Jer. 52:28 ff. we have an extract from an official document of the Babylonian *golah* giving exact figures for the three deportations, whose total is there computed at only 4,600 souls. The number of those exiled in 598 is set at 3,023 instead of 8,000 (or 10,000) in Kings; the difference may be partly due to the fact that the latter was only a conjectural estimate, but may also be partly due to the heavy mortality of the starving and diseased captives during the long desert trek to Babylonia. There, however, the native energy and capacity of the captives quickly asserted themselves. In recently published tablets from a royal archive of Nebuchadnezzar, dating in and about the year 592 B.C., Jehoiachin and five of his sons, as well as at least five other Jews, are mentioned among recipients of rations from the royal court. It is significant that Jehoiachin was still called "king of Judah" in official Babylonian documents.[173]

Just as Jeremiah had denounced the wickedness of Judah, urging his people to bow to the Chaldean yoke, so did his younger contemporary, Ezekiel, in the Babylonian *golah*, whose focus (outside of Babylon) was at a colony established on the Chebar Canal near Nippur in central Babylonia.[174] In spite of the corrupt text of his poems and prose sermons, their purport is clear almost throughout. The Prophet depicted the religious perversity of the men of Judah in scathing terms, employing figures of unexcelled vividness. He predicted the downfall of the state and the captivity of its population, just as Jeremiah was doing in Jerusalem. From the Jews in exile he demanded puritanical standards of morality, strict accountability of the individual for his actions, and rigid monotheism. It is significant that we hear no more of pagan practices among the Babylonian Jews, whereas the Egyptian Jews who had flouted Jeremiah, as well as many Yahwists in Northern Israel and Trans-Jordan during the next century, practiced syncretistic rites which at best compromised seriously with the surrounding paganism.

It is now possible, thanks to archaeological discoveries, to reconstruct the situation of the Jews in Palestine during the

Exile with general clarity. All, or virtually all, of the fortified towns in Judah had been razed to the ground as thoroughly as we know to have been the case at Debir, Lachish, Beth-shemesh and Beth-haccherem (Ramat Rahel). (We mention only those sites which have been adequately excavated; the evidence is clear for many other sites from soundings and surface exploration.) We are expressly told that the Chaldean general, Nabu-zer-iddin, left many of the poor in order to harvest grapes and make wine (Jerusalem was captured early in the grape harvest). On the other hand, a number of the Jewish settlements in the Negeb (which seems to have been detached from the Judahite state in 597 B.C.) appear to have escaped destruction, and the Israelite towns north of the old border remained under Babylonian control, being thus saved from the fate of the towns to the south: Bethel, for example, was occupied through this period and down probably into the middle or late sixth century. So also was Tell en-Nasbeh (Ataroth). The territory belonging to Judah in 589 was divided between the Edomites (Idumeans), who settled in the southern hill-country about Adoraim (Dura) and Hebron, and the Babylonian province of Samaria (as shown by Albrecht Alt).[175] There was also a considerable Israelite population in Ephraim, Galilee and Trans-Jordan; and at some time before the middle of the fifth century Yahwists became hereditary governors of Samaria and Ammon.

As long as the exiled king lived there was hope for a restoration of the Jewish monarchy, and this hope appears to have flamed up brightly when the news of Jehoiachin's release from prison after the death of Nebuchadnezzar was circulated through the *golah* (captivity) (561 B.C.). It is not likely that there was a long interval between Jehoiachin's death and the fall of the Chaldean Empire under the onslaught of Cyrus in 539. His three older sons, all born before 592 (as shown by recently published cuneiform documents)[176] were probably already dead by this time, leaving his fourth son, who bore the well-attested Babylonian name Sin-ab-usur,[177] to head the Davidic family and to enter into negotiations with the Persians for a restoration of the Jewish state. The enthusiastic resurgence of Jewish nationalism on a deeper religious basis, which we find at this time, is eloquently portrayed by Deutero-Isaiah, who combined Jewish nationalism with religious universalism; nowhere in earlier prophetic literature do we find such explicit recognition of the gulf existing between the One God, whose special favor had been extended to Israel, and the nonexistent deities who were mistakenly worshiped by the Gentile peoples. In this stage of the Zionism of the Restoration, there was a pure religious idealism which reminds one in certain respects of the cultural idealism of Ahad Ha-Am and Eliezer ben Yehuda in the generation before the First World War.

The substantial historicity of the Edict of Cyrus (Ezra 1:2-4; 6:3-5) in 538 has been confirmed by modern archaeological discoveries,[178] but it is wholly unnecessary to suppose that it was followed by any wide response on the part of the Jews of the *golah*. In the first place, the latter were in general becoming well established in their new homes, as vividly illustrated by Egyptian papyri beginning in the year 495 and by Babylonian contract tablets dating from various periods (but sporadic and often uncertain until 437 B.C., when Jewish names become abundant in the Nippur documents).[179] In the second place, the journey was dangerous and expensive, while conditions in Judah were certainly very unsatisfactory. However, between 538 and the death of the Persian king Cambyses in 522 many Jews had undoubtedly returned to Palestine, among them Zerubbabel, son of Jehoiachin's eldest son, Shealtiel, who had replaced his uncle Sin-ab-usur as head of the Davidic house, and the high priest, Joshua (Jeshua). They found a very small territory to call their own, stretching less than twenty-five miles in a straight line along the watershed ridge from north of Jerusalem to south of Beth-zur, with a total population which can scarcely have exceeded 20,000 in 522 B.C.[180] The governors and nobles of Samaria, who had regarded this district as part of their province, were openly hostile. On the other hand, there were extensive districts in Greater Palestine which were peopled wholly or partly by Jews and Israelites, and a modest flow of capital was assured by immigrants and gifts to the Holy Place.

Zerubbabel (Zer-Babil, "Offspring of Babylon," a common

Babylonian name), whose father had been born about 597
(as we know from recent finds), was not an impetuous youth,
as generally assumed, but a cautious man of middle age (almost certainly born before 570). His caution irritated the fiery
prophets, Haggai and Zechariah, who seized the opportunity
offered by the continuous rebellions in every part of the Persian Empire which followed the accession of Darius Hystaspes
in December, 522, or January, 521. Haggai's first oracle was
not delivered until August, 520; in it he spurred the men of
Judah to take up the long overdue rebuilding of the Temple
in earnest. Less than a month later work actually began.
Haggai's second oracle (Hag. 2: 1 ff.), nearly two months
later, proclaims the approaching downfall of Persia and the
coming of a new Jewish state; in his fourth oracle (Hag.
2:20 ff.), dated in December, he explicitly declared that the
imperial throne would be overturned and implied that Zerubbabel was the Lord's anointed.[181] Most of Zechariah's prophecies are later, reflecting the situation that followed the complete triumph of Darius over his foes, when the ambiguous
stand of the Jews during the previous year naturally became
the target of official Persian investigation. Whether Zerubbabel died a natural death or was removed, we cannot say;
there is not the slightest reason to suppose that he committed
any overt act of disloyalty to the crown. In spite of the hostility
of the satrap of Syria and the men of Samaria, the Temple was
finished in March, 515; evidently the Persian authorities con-
tented themselves with depriving the Davidic family of its
political prerogatives, which were turned over to Joshua
(Jeshua) and his successors. We may safely credit Joshua with
political astuteness in the difficult situation in which he found
himself.

The disappointment felt by Jews in all parts of the Persian
Empire at the failure of the restored Davidic state to ma-
terialize must have been followed, just as in similar recent
situations, by decline in their interest in Judah. This shift of
interest left the little priestly state of Judah unable for three
generations greatly to influence currents of Jewish life in other
parts of the world. Meanwhile Jewish communities were being
founded in cities as remote from Jerusalem as Sardis, capital

of Lydia.[182] It is true that the Temple had been rebuilt, but efforts to reconstruct the ancient city walls had been thwarted by the officials of Samaria, and Jerusalem was surrounded with ruins. In this period of some sixty years, however, the population may have doubled, and more or less normal relations between the returned exiles and the older Jewish population were certainly established. The time was ripe for a new forward step in the resurrection of Zion.

FROM NEHEMIAH TO THE FALL
OF THE PERSIAN EMPIRE

It may appear strange but it is nevertheless true that the history of the Jews in the fifth century B.C. is in some respects more obscure than any corresponding section of Israel's history after the twelfth century B.C. This is due to the fact that the books of Ezra and Nehemiah have undergone unusual vicissitudes, leaving their text and the order of their contents in quite extraordinary confusion, with sharply divergent recensions to warn us against docilely following any one. It is scarcely surprising that distinguished biblical scholars have dated Ezra and Nehemiah in almost every part of the period covered by this section, or that opinions differ widely as to the order of their careers. Nor is it altogether surprising that the Ezra Memoirs were declared by Charles C. Torrey and others to be quite apocryphal. Thanks to archaeological discoveries, particularly the Elephantine Papyri (since 1906) and the Jehoiachin tablets (1939; see above), we can now date Nehemiah in the third quarter of the fifth century with certainty and can locate Ezra with a high degree of confidence shortly after him. Our arguments and those of our precursors will be found elsewhere; here we can sketch only the results, with emphasis on the degree of probability in each case.[183]

Among the personalities of ancient history there are few which present themselves to us as vividly as that of Nehemiah, thanks to his *apologia pro vita sua*, whose authenticity has never been doubted by any scholar of competence. Endowed with unusual energy and presumably with exceptional charm, he rose to a high rank among the court officials of Artaxerxes Longimanus (465-424), whose cupbearer he became. As long since recognized, this position required a eunuch to fill it, and there is strong collateral evidence in favor of such an interpretation of Nehemiah's career.[184] His love for his people was so great, however, that his physical handicap became an asset and he was able to serve Israel with rare single-mindedness. On the other hand, the petulance and obstinacy that formed the reverse side of his character made it difficult for him to collaborate, and he made bitter enemies.

It appears to have been in December, 445, that Nehemiah learned from his brother Hanani and other Jews who had recently come from Jerusalem how bad the situation there really was. He seems to have been particularly moved by the news that the walls were still in ruins (see above), a fact which made it possible for Arab, Edomite or Ammonite raiders to attack the unprotected Holy City almost at will. It was apparently not until considerably later that he succeeded in arousing the interest of the king in the plight of the Jews in Palestine. To judge from the additional details preserved by Josephus, Nehemiah did not actually arrive in Palestine, armed with a bodyguard and royal rescripts, until the year 440.[185] Early in August, 439, he began the work of rebuilding the great city wall, almost exactly 148 years after its destruction by the Chaldeans (if our chronology is correct). Fifty-two days later, thanks to energetic efforts on his part and to a mass levy from all parts of the little province of Judea, the wall had been raised. However, work on the wall cannot actually have been completed in such a short time by volunteer workmen; and we may safely follow the explicit statement of Josephus that the entire work took two years and four months, especially since the latter fixes the start of the work in a month which agrees exactly with the month given by the Hebrew text for its beginning. If Josephus was right, the task of finishing the battlements, of building great revetments, towers, gates, etc., was not completed until December, 437.[186]

Nehemiah's personal relationships were not so happy as one might expect from this brilliant initial success. That he was bitterly opposed by Sin-uballit (Sanballat), governor of Samaria, was only natural, since the latter had fallen heir to the old claims of Samaria on the territory of Judah, which had belonged to it during Chaldean times, as shown by Albrecht Alt.[187] Sin-uballit, in spite of his inherited Babylonian name, was a Yahwist by religion, as proved by the fact that two of his sons were named Delaiah and Shelemiah; some of his hostility may be traced to the machinations of hostile groups among the priests, prophets and nobles of Judea, about which Nehemiah complains so bitterly in his memoirs. Tobiah, governor of Ammon, who controlled central Trans-Jordan, also was hostile to Nehemiah; his Yahwism is proved by his own name, that of his son, Johanan, and the fact that his descendants in the early second century B.C. were still Jews.[188] That the Yahwism of Sin-uballit and Tobiah was not that of the returned exiles in Jerusalem, much less that of the Babylonian *golah*, may be considered as certain, especially after the Elephantine discoveries; it was a syncretistic structure with archaic features, presumably something like the religion of the Jewish colonists at Elephantine.[189]

An excellent idea of the population and social organization of Judea in the time of Nehemiah is provided by the census list in Neh. 7 (and Ezra 2), which may represent the original list of returned exiles, with corrected numbers and additional entries to bring it up to date.[190] It is composed of two main groups: the returned exiles and their descendants; the inhabitants of towns in northern Judea whose forebears had presumably returned to their homes not long after the Chaldean invasion or who had never left them. Among the former are a number of families whose names prove their late origin, as is particularly clear in the case of the family of Bagoi (Bigvai), bearing a characteristic Iranian name, but also in the case of the family of Elam (evidently descended from settlers in the region around Susa) and of the family of the "Governor of Moab" (Pahath-moab).[191] Among the latter are such Judahite towns as Bethlehem and Netophah, Benjamite towns such as Ramah and Geba, and also Ephraimite towns (north of the pre-exilic border) like Bethel and Ai; farther away were Jericho and a little group of three towns of Ephraim on the edge of the Plain of Sharon around Lod (Lydda). Since Bethzur, Keilah, Tekoa and other towns of Judah farther south, mentioned in the account of Nehemiah's building operations, do not appear in this census, it seems clear that this part of the

province was virtually uninhabited when the exiles began to
return after 538 B.C. On the other hand, the region around
Jerusalem was already settled and offered less room for the
returning Jews. Archaeological work at Bethel has proved
that it was occupied down to the middle or latter part of the
sixth century, and was then destroyed by a great conflagration;
it was later reoccupied but remained thinly settled down into
the third century B.C.[192] Lydda and the adjoining towns may
have been added to the province by Nehemiah himself. Jerusalem was peopled mainly by priests, Levites and Nethinim,
etc., as well as by a certain number of officials and tradesmen.
The total population of Judah was over 42,000 freeborn Jews,
besides over 7,000 slaves and menials, approximately 50,000 in
all, of whom between 10,000 and 15,000 may have lived in
and around the capital. While this was only a tiny nucleus for
a Jewish state, it was already a respectable development for
about a century of growth from extremely small beginnings.

Unfortunately, as indicated above, we are very unsatisfac-
torily informed about the date of Ezra. The most recent evidence favors a date for Ezra's mission in or about the thirty-
seventh year of Artaxerxes, *i.e.*, about 428 B.C.[193] It is not
clear whether Nehemiah was in Jerusalem at the time; he is
not specifically mentioned in the Ezra Memoirs proper, and
the evidence is conflicting.[194] There can, however, be little
doubt that his influence was directly responsible for the royal
rescript giving Ezra extensive powers in connection with his
plan to reform the religious organization at Jerusalem. The
view, brilliantly defended by Eduard Meyer and Hans Hein-
rich Schaeder,[195] that "Judaism was created by the Persian
Empire," is exaggerated, and has, in fact, no more real validity
than the corresponding statement, sometimes heard, that
"Zionism was created by the British." We need not underesti-
mate the role played by Cyrus and Nehemiah, by Lord Bal-
four and Lord Samuel, to recognize that in general there was
more opposition than support among Persian and British officials. Judaism and Zionism were both developed by the Jewish
people, working against great odds—so great, in fact, that
without benevolent assistance at critical moments from the

Persian and British imperial authorities success might have been impossible, in spite of the determination of the leaders of both movements.

Nowhere in the Ezra Memoirs proper is there a clear statement about who was then *tirshatha* (royal commissioner) of Judea, but we may safely infer that it was Nehemiah himself, whose brother Hanani (Hananiah) may have taken charge during his absence (cf. Neh. 7:2). It is noteworthy that the latter was still apparently at the head of Jewish affairs in Jerusalem a few years later in 419, when an edict of Arsames, Persian viceroy of Babylonia, Syria and Egypt, with regard to the orthodox observance of Passover, was forwarded through him to the Jewish colonists at Elephantine.[196] Nor have we any information about what happened between Nehemiah's governorship and the year 411 B.C., when we find a Persian, one Bagoas (Bagohi), named in official documents as governor of Judea, while the chief political role under him reverts to the high priest. In Nehemiah's time Eliashib, grandson of Joshua, who must have been well along in years, was high priest (until after 433 B.C.). When Ezra came to Jerusalem a few years later, Eliashib's grandson Johanan seems already to have been high priest (cf. Ezra 10:6 with Neh. 11:23). The latter was still high priest in 408, but by that time he had probably lost the respect of all by murdering his brother Joshua in the Temple, an act which shocked the world of that day and brought severe reprisals from Bagoas. Not long afterwards he was succeeded by his son Jedaiah (Jaddua), with whom our knowledge of the succession of high priests stops until the Hellenistic period.

Ezra's greatest significance in the history of Judaism probably lay in the field of cultic reform rather than in that of political action. He seems to have played an important role in establishing the canonical Torah as the normative rule of Israel's faith. The Pentateuch was probably edited in approximately its present form by an orthodox Jewish circle in Babylonia, employing the so-called JE document from the early Monarchy, the Deuteronomic Code from the end of the Monarchy, and the Priestly Code. The last-named component of the Pentateuch represents the official tradition of the patriarchal age, the Mosaic period and the ritual law of the Tabernacle as handed down by the priests of the Temple in Jerusalem. It contains some very early material, much of it probably written long before the Exile. As it stands, however, P may have been put into approximately its present form during the seventh century B.C. The first four books were probably edited in substantially their present form during the Exile, but it seems likely that it was Ezra who introduced the complete Pentateuch into normative Jewish use and who was partly responsible for the way in which its archaic practices were adjusted to actual ritual usage in the Temple. The latter was alone a major contribution to the future of normative Judaism.

In another direction we may credit Ezra with original literary compilation. We owe to Charles C. Torrey recognition of the fact that the style and point of view of the Ezra Memoirs (in which Ezra speaks primarily in the first person) are identical with those of the Chronicler.[197] It is, therefore, highly probable that Jewish tradition is in principle correct in identifying Ezra with the Chronicler. Since the first edition of the latter's work brings us down to the time of Johanan, and since (as we may now affirm with confidence) his genealogy of the Davidic house closes before the end of the fifth century,[198] there is no historical improbability in this tradition. All internal and linguistic objections to dating the final redaction of the Chronicler's work after the early fourth century have been disproved by recent archaeological research.[199]

The fourth century is almost wholly without dated Jewish documents. Egypt and Babylonia cease to yield any information about the further fortunes of the Jewish colonies, regarding which we were so well informed in the latter part of the fifth century. In Judah we lack even the names of the high priests after Jaddua, though we may suspect that the names of a Johanan and a second Jaddua have dropped out of later lists. On the other hand, archaeology has demonstrated that the Jewish state of the fourth century was recognized by the Persian authorities as a hierocratic commonwealth like that of Hierapolis in northern Syria. Judah also enjoyed the right to levy its own taxes and to strike its own silver coins—employing the *darkemah* standard (imitating, as E. L. Sukenik has shown, contemporary Attic drachmas) which is attested in the work of the Chronicler.[200] The material culture of Jewish Palestine was already saturated with Greek influence,[201] which was soon to engulf the world and to usher in a new era, fraught with both evil and good.

NOTES

1. It is true that the Greek translation of the third century B.C. renders simply "in the land of the Chaldeans," omitting any reference to Ur. Yet the Book of Jubilees, which is probably only slightly later (cf. most recently *From the Stone Age to Christianity*, 1957 ed., p. 20), mentions both an eponymous hero named "Ur son of Kesed," who "built Ara (misunderstood Aramaic *arʿa*, "land"?) of the Chaldeans," and Ur of the Chaldees itself (the latter repeatedly). It therefore seems to me that the most probable solution is to be sought in a different direction: the original Hebrew text may have been "Ur (in the) land of the Chaldees," which was differently abbreviated by haplography in the recensions underlying the Septuagint and the Masoretic text. Cf. my discussion in *Bull. Am. Sch. Or. Res.*, No. 140, pp. 31 f.
2. See my remarks and references in *From the Stone Age to Christianity*, 1957 ed., pp. 236 ff.
3. Cf. n. 2, as well as J. Lewy in the *Revue de l'Histoire des Religions*, 1934, pp. 44 ff.
4. See *Jour. Bib. Lit.*, LVIII (1939), pp. 91-103.
5. According to this cycle of legends (which I hope to discuss at a convenient opportunity) Babylon was built just "opposite" Accad, capital of Sargon I, who established a mighty empire in the twenty-third century B.C. Its name *Babili(m)*, "Gate of God" (of which *Kadingirra* is merely the Sumerian translation), and other points in the story indicate that it was an important shrine, whose temple tower was perhaps the highest (and earliest?) structure of the kind to be erected in that age. We now know that Accad was located just south of Babylon on the ancient course of the Euphrates.
6. Cf. the preceding references, to which add *Bull. Am. Sch. Or. Res.*, No. 83, p. 34.
7. For the Mari archives in general cf. *Bull. Am. Sch. Or. Res.*, Nos. 77, pp. 20 ff., and 78, pp. 23 ff., as well as G. E. Mendenhall, *Bib. Arch.*, XI (1948), pp. 1-19. On the two last items in the paragraph see G. Dossin, *Revue d'Assyriologie*, XXXVI, 50 ff., XXXV, 174 ff. (cf. *Ancient Near Eastern Texts Relating to the Old Testament*, ed. J. B. Pritchard [hereafter *ANET*], p. 482).
8. On the demographic history of Trans-Jordan see Nelson Glueck, *The Other Side of the Jordan*, pp. 20 ff.

9. See *Bull. Am. Sch. Or. Res.*, Nos., 81, pp. 16 ff., and 83, pp. 30 ff.

10. See J. A. Wilson, *Am. Jour. Sem. Lang.*, LVIII (1941), 225-236, as well as my remarks in *The Bible and the Ancient Near East* (1961), pp. 332 ff.

11. See my observations in *Archaeology and the Religion of Israel*, pp. 98 f., 200, as well as N. Avigad, *Bull. Am. Sch. Or. Res.*, No. 163, pp. 18 ff.

12. Cf. Alt, *Kleine Schriften*, I, pp. 141 ff.

13. For a comprehensive account, with bibliography, see C. H. Gordon, *Bib. Arch.*, III (1940), 1-12.

14. On this subject cf. my observations, *From the Stone Age to Christianity*, 1957 ed., pp. 64 ff.

15. Cf. *Bull. Am. Sch. Or. Res.*, No. 163, pp. 36-54.

16. *Ibid.*, pp. 53-54. A detailed paper on the subject is in preparation, with material from Sumerian, Accadian, Ugaritic, Egyptian and other sources.

17. First correctly recognized by R. Borger, *Zeits. Deutsch. Paläst.-Ver.*, LXXIV (1958), pp. 130 ff. In Syriac, *'afir* (*'appir*), from original *'apir*, with two short vowels.

18. See above, n. 1.

19. Cf. *Bull. Am. Sch. Or. Res.*, No. 163, pp. 44-48.

20. See Y. Aharoni, *Israel Explor. Jour.*, 4 (1954), pp. 34 f.

21. Cf. *Bull. Am. Sch. Or. Res.*, No. 163, pp. 41 f.

22. *Ibid.*, p. 38, n. 9, with the references there. For Walz's still unpublished paper on ass nomadism, see the abstract which appeared in the *Akten* of the 1957 (Munich) International Congress of Orientalists (Wiesbaden, 1959), pp. 150-152.

23. Cf. *Bull. Am. Sch. Or. Res.*, No. 163, pp. 49 ff., and the previous discussions listed on p. 49, n. 66.

24. *Ibid.*, pp. 46 f. Cf. also M. F. Unger, *Israel and the Aramaeans of Damascus*, pp. 3 f.

25. Cf. *Bull. Am. Sch. Or. Res.*, No. 121, pp. 21 f. The men whose names are listed belong to the class called *ashannu* at Alalakh; the first two signs are found in one text, the last one in the other.

26. See in particular Ian Cunnison, "History and Genealogies in a Conquest State," *Amer. Anthropologist*, 59 (1957), pp. 20-31, and R. C. Suggs, "Historical Traditions and Archaeology in Polynesia," *ibid.*, 62 (1960), pp. 764-773. There is a good deal of material from modern Arabian genealogies which points in the same direction. The writer has not yet published his own collections from South Arabia, where the same phenomenon appears.

27. See *Bull. Am. Sch. Or. Res.*, No. 140, pp. 31 f.

28. Cf. *From the Stone Age to Christianity*, 1957 ed., pp. 242 f.

29. See *Bull. Am. Sch. Or. Res.*, No. 99, pp. 13-17.

30. Cf. my remarks in *The Bible and the Ancient Near East*, pp. 335 ff.

31. See above, n. 16.

32. Cf. *From the Stone Age to Christianity*, 1957 ed., 212, 223 f.; *Bull. Am. Sch. Or. Res.*, No. 84, pp. 7-11.

33. See *Bull. Am. Sch. Or. Res.*, No. 110, pp. 6 ff.

34. See *Lachish IV: The Bronze Age*, Pls. 37 and 38, No. 295.

35. I expect to discuss this name soon; it occurs on a figurine from a tomb of the late fourteenth century B.C. excavated by Petrie (see his *Kahun, Gurob, Hawara*, Pl. 24), and was identified in 1910 by Burchardt (this identification is strikingly confirmed by my phonetic study of New Empire transcriptions).

36. See my discussion, *Jour. Bib. Lit.*, LIV (1935), pp. 180-193; see also M. Weippert, *Zeits. Deutsch. Morg. Ges.*, CXI (1961), pp. 42-62. I have much unpublished material in support of my original view.

37. Cf. Meek, *Am. Jour. Sem. Lang.*, LVI (1939), 113-120.

38. On the identification of Tanis with Rameses (Raamses) see Montet, *Géographie de l'Égypte ancienne*, I, pp. 192 ff.

39. Cf. Alan Rowe, *The Topography and History of Beth-Shan*, p. 34, and Wilson, in *ANET*, p. 255.

40. Cf. *From the Stone Age to Christianity*, 1957 ed., pp. 218 ff., 269 f.

41. *Ibid.*, p. 223; see further A. H. Gardiner, *Hieratic Papyri in the British Museum*, Third Series, I, pp. 28-37, and Adolf Erman, "Der Leidener Amonshymnus," *Sitz. Preuss. Akad. Wiss.*, 1923; see also Wilson in *ANET*, pp. 368 f., 371 f.

42. Cf. *Archaeology and the Religion of Israel*, pp. 77, 86. See also especially Marvin Pope, *Wörterbuch der Mythologie* I, 2, pp. 235-241.

43. See Wilson in *ANET*, pp. 34 ff.

44. See my paper, *Jour. Bib. Lit.*, LXIII (1944), pp. 207-233.

45. For Elyon see Levi della Vida, *Jour. Bib. Lit.*, 63 (1944), pp. 1-9; see further, M. Pope, *op. cit.*, I, 2, pp. 283 f. For Eli see M. Dahood, *Theol. Stud.*, XIV (1953), pp. 452 ff.

46. A striking Greek case may serve to illustrate how a block of laws from the original code (now known only from Ex. 21-23 and a few fragments elsewhere) may have survived after the rest was lost. Professor John H. Kent of Southwestern (Memphis) has called my attention to the fact that the only block of legislation from the Attic code of Draco (*c.* 621 B.C.) which has survived to our time is a group of laws about homicide, re-enacted in 409-408 and inscribed at that time on stone; see Bonner and Smith, *The Administration of Justice from Homer to Aristotle*, I, pp. 110 and *passim*. For the various codes see *ANET*, pp. 159-197.

47. See Alt, "Ursprünge des israelitischen Rechts," *Kleine Schriften*, I, pp. 278-332. For earlier Hittite analogies see G. E. Mendenhall, *Law and Covenant in Israel and the Ancient Near East*, pp. 6 f.

48. Cf. *Jour. Bib. Lit.*, LXIII (1944), pp. 227 ff.

49. Cf. A Bergman, *Jour. Pal. Or. Soc.*, 1936, pp. 224-254.

50. R. H. Pfeiffer, *Introduction to the Old Testament* (1941), p. 281.

51. Cf. *Heb. Un. Coll. Annual*, XXIII, i (1950-51), pp. 7 f., n. 17.

52. Cf. *Festschrift für A. Bertholet* (1950), pp. 1 ff. Cf. Psa. 48:2 f., where the mountain at the "back of the north, the city of the great king," though in a completely monotheistic Israelite context, goes back to Mount Casius as the seat of Baal. As in so much of the Psalter, the ancient imagery has been demythologized.

53. Cf. *Jour. Am. Or. Soc.*, 74 (1954), p. 233.

54. See Montet, *Le drame d'Avaris* (Paris, 1941), and my remarks on chronology, *Bull. Am. Sch. Or. Res.*, No. 99, pp. 13 ff. See also n. 38 above.

55. See my remarks in *The Archaeology of Palestine* (1960), pp. 106 f.

56. See I. Mendelsohn, *Bull. Am. Sch. Or. Res.*, No. 83, pp. 36-39; E. R. Lacheman, *ibid.*, No. 86, pp. 36 f. See also E. A. Speiser, *Jour. Am. Or. Soc.*, 74 (1954), p. 21.

57. Cf. *Bull. Am. Sch. Or. Res.*, No. 163, pp. 53 f.

58. Cf. Y. Yadin, *Isr. Expl. Jour.*, 8 (1958), pp. 280 f., and *Bibl. Arch.*, XXII (1959), pp. 2 ff.

59. Cf. K. Kenyon, *Archaeology in the Holy Land* (1960), pp. 209 ff. (see also G. E. Wright, *Biblical Archaeology*, pp. 78 ff.). Her date for the end of the Late Bronze phase, *c.* 1325 B.C. (p. 211) reckons only with the painted Canaanite sherds under the "hillani" structure of the tenth century B.C., which are relatively early (cf. Wright, *Bull. Am. Sch. Or. Res.*, No. 86, pp. 32 ff.), and not with the Mycenaean vases and imitations from Tomb 13 and the outside of the glacis, which were correctly dated by Garstang in the thirteenth century B.C. (*The Story of Jericho*, 2nd. ed., pp. 127 f.). They are definitely Late Helladic III A.

60. This date is considerably earlier than my previous estimates, which usually allowed for a date not later than *c.* 2200 B.C. Repeated study of the pottery published by Judith Marquet-Krause (1949) has convinced me that none of it is later than the middle of the third millennium. We now know, thanks to still unpublished discoveries of J. L. Kelso at Bethel, that the latter site was already occupied in part during the period of Khirbet Kerak ware, none of which was found at Ai.

61. See *Bull. Am. Sch. Or. Res.*, No. 74, pp. 16 f.

62. See provisionally *Bull. Am. Sch. Or. Res.*, No. 56, pp. 6 ff. The work done by the writer and J. L. Kelso in 1934 has been continued in recent years by Kelso, who has found additional evidence for the thirteenth century date. The final report is now almost ready for the press.

63. The name almost certainly comes from Hebrew *luz*, "to hide, to be hidden," etc., with the Arabic cognate *ladha*, "to elude, shift, take refuge" (*maladh*, "place of refuge"). Hugo Winckler had already seen this in principle (*Geschichte Israels*, II, p. 65).

64. The tombs have so far been published only in the *Illustrated London News*. The sherds were seen by the writer in Berkeley, thanks to Pritchard's courtesy.

65. For a relatively minimal estimate of the historical role of Joshua see Alt, "Joshua," in *Kleine Schriften*, I, pp. 176-192, followed by Noth, *The History of Israel* (1958), pp. 92 f. For a relatively maximal view see *Bull. Am. Sch. Or. Res.*, No. 74, pp. 12 ff., and G. E. Wright, *Jour. Near East. Stud.*, V (1946), pp. 105-114.

66. See *Jour. Bib. Lit.*, LXIII (1944), pp. 207-233, *Bull. Am. Sch. Or. Res.*, No. 118, pp. 15 f., n. 13.

67. See *From the Stone Age to Christianity*, 1957 ed., p. 20.

68. Besides the many references in the Amarna tablets, we have a reference in the second Sethos stele from Beth-shan, which dates from about 1300 B.C.; see *Bull. Am. Sch. Or. Res.*, No. 125, pp. 24-32.

69. Cf. a forthcoming paper of G. E. Mendenhall in *Bib. Arch.*, which is independent of my own treatment (in manuscript since 1958 but not yet published).

70. On this group see J. R. Kupper, *Les nomades en Mésopotamie au temps des rois de Mari* (1957), pp. 47-81. The group *TUR-ya-mi-na* must be read *Bin-Yamina* and *TUR.MES-ya-mi-na* is to be read *Banu-Yamina* as shown clearly by the contrasting *TUR.MES-Si-im-a-al*, to be read *Banu-Sim'al*. Since both of the second elements are good Northwest-Semitic words, it is incredible that *TUR* was read as Accadian (*mar*), especially since *binu*, "son," is attested in Accadian.

71. See above, n. 61. Cf. also Z. Kallai-Kleinmann, *Encyclopedia Biblica* (Jerusalem), II, cols. 54 ff., who points out that Hos. 5:8, which is obviously very archaic, mentions Beth-aven as one of the three most important towns of Benjamin.

72. For some details with regard to Canaanite religion and mythology see *Archaeology and the Religion of Israel*, pp. 68-94; *From the Stone Age to Christianity*, 1957 ed., pp. 230-236; also M. Dahood, "Ancient Semitic Deities in Syria and Palestine," in S. Moscati, *Le antiche divinità semitiche*, pp. 65-94, and M. Pope and W. Röllig, *Wörterbuch der Mythologie*, I, 2, pp. 219-312.

73. See especially Noth, *Das System der Zwölf Stämme Israels* (1930); *History of Israel*, pp. 85 ff. Cf. *Archaeology and the Religion of Israel*, pp. 102 ff.

74. Cf. G. E. Mendenhall, *Law and Covenant in Israel and the Ancient Near East*, pp. 41 f. See also the review by W. L. Moran, *Biblica*, 1960, pp. 297 ff.

75. On the geographical and historical role of the Jordan see Nelson Glueck, *The River Jordan* (1946).

76. Cf. the statement of the official record in the Papyrus Harris (Wilson, in *ANET*, p. 262). They were probably employed as slave or mercenary troops; cf. H. H. Nelson, *Early Historical Records of Ramses III*, p. 4, n. 24, and the admirable treatment by Trude Dothan, *Antiquity and Survival*, II, 2/3 (1957), pp. 151-164.

77. See my discussion in *Tell Beit Mirsim*, I, pp. 53 ff., *Tell Beit Mirsim*, III, pp. 1 ff., 36 ff.; Elihu Grant and G. E. Wright, *Ain Shems Excavations*, V, pp. 126 ff.

78. See the writer in *Studies Presented to David Moore Robinson* (1951), I, pp. 223 ff., and J. Černý, *Rev. Égypt.*, 6, p. 41, n. 18, who insists that it is an actual report, not merely a literary composition. See also his *Paper and Books in Ancient Egypt* (University College London, 1952), p. 22.

79. See *Tell Beit Mirsim*, III, pp. 36 f.

80. Both in the Song and in the prose narrative which precedes (Judg. 3:31), Shamgar definitely antedates the events described in the Song and is explicitly said to have routed the Philistines.

81. Cf. already my discussion in *Jour. Pal. Or. Soc.*, 1921, pp. 60 f. The name is later attested as that of a family of temple attendants, among whom are a number of certain non-Hebrew names, including one Egyptian and one Edomite name (Ezra 2:53; Neh. 7:55), with the same Hebrew consonants attested in the Greek transcriptions.

82. In 1937 (*Bull. Am. Sch. Or. Res.*, No. 68), following study of the Megiddo excavations on the spot, I concluded that the Song of Deborah should be dated in the period when the town was in ruins, between Megiddo VII and VI, since Judg. 5:19 locates the battle "at Taanach, by the Waters of Megiddo," thus implying that Megiddo itself was not occupied at the time. In 1940 I withdrew from my position, accepting Engberg's date between VI and V, in the early eleventh century (*ibid.*, No. 78, pp. 4-9). Since then, J. Simons (*Oudtestamentische Studien*, I [1942], pp. 38-54) has also argued that the break between VI and V was more significant than that between VII and VI. After studying *Megiddo II* (1948), as well as the pottery from the Megiddo excavations, I withdrew my acceptance of Engberg's view and returned to my original position. The break between VII and VI was much more complete and more protracted than that between VI and V, while the change in character of masonry and pottery also was much greater.

83. The confusion in Judg. 4, as well as in modern treatments of this episode, was presumably caused originally by identification of Jabin, king of Hazor in the time of Joshua, with a later Canaanite prince of the same name who followed Shamgar and was probably involved in the coalition against Israel described in Judg. 5. The name *Yabin* is an easily explicable phonetic development from a more original *Yabn(i)*. The name *Yabn(i)* itself is a typical short form (hypocoristic) of original *Yabni-El* or *Yabni-Hadad*. This type of name was very common in Bronze Age Palestine; in fact, the name of a prince of Hazor in the Mari texts is Yabni-Hadad (Babylonian Ibni-Adad).

84. Cf. *From the Stone Age to Christianity*, 1957 ed., pp. 215 ff., and Max Weber, *Ancient Judaism*, pp. 40, 83 ff.

85. Cf. the writer, *loc. cit.*

86. See above, n. 22.

87. Otto Eissfeldt, *Das Lied Moses Deuteronomium 32 1-43* etc. (1958).

88. See the writer's Goldenson Lecture for 1961, *Samuel and the Beginnings of the Prophetic Movement* (Hebrew Union College Press, Cincinnati).

89. See F. M. Cross, Jr., *Bull. Am. Sch. Or. Res.*, No. 132, pp. 15 ff.

90. The Hebrew of Ecclus. 46:13 has *nazir* YYY, i.e., Nazirite of God. This is omitted in the Greek text, which diverges unusually far from the Hebrew text at this point.

91. Cf. *Samuel and the Beginnings of the Prophetic Movement*, pp. 19-21, for a number of striking examples from the past twenty-one centuries.

92. See *ibid.*, pp. 7 ff., for the significance of the ecstatic movement.

93. Cf. P. W. Skehan, *Bull. Am. Sch. Or. Res.*, No. 136, pp. 12 ff.; *Jour. Bib. Lit.*, LXXVIII (1959), p. 22. On the archaism of the poem see my discussion in *Vetus Test.*, IX (1959), pp. 339-346.

94. Cf. *Samuel and the Beginnings of the Prophetic Movement*, pp. 23 ff.

95. See my remarks in *Miscellanea Biblica B. Ubach* (1954), pp. 131-136.

96. See B. Maisler (Mazar), *Bull. Am. Sch. Or. Res.*, No. 102, p. 10, and my discussion in *The Bible and the Ancient Near East*, pp. 342 ff.

97. See J. A. Fitzmyer, *Catholic Bibl. Quart.*, 20 (1958), pp. 448, 450, 459. The word *ngdy*, "my commanders," appears between *bny*, "my sons," and *pqdy*, "my officials." Cf. also my *Samuel and the Beginnings of the Prophetic Movement*, pp. 15 f.

98. See J. A. Sanders, *Bull. Am. Sch. Or. Res.*, No. 165, p. 15.

99. *Annual Am. Sch. Or. Res.*, IV (1924); *Bull. Am. Sch. Or. Res.*, No. 52, pp. 6-12; L. Sinclair, *Annual Am. Sch. Or. Res.*, XXXIV (1954-56), pp. 10 ff.

100. See provisionally *Archaeology and the Religion of Israel*, pp. 125-129.

101. Cf. *Tell Beit Mirsim*, III, pp. 12 ff., 37. Y. Aharoni (*Bull. Am. Sch. Or. Res.*, No. 154, pp. 35-39) thinks the casemate walls in question were Solomonic, because of the resemblance of their structure to Solomonic Hazor. In view of the fact that Solomonic masonry tends to be much better than the casemate walls of Tell Beit Mirsim and Beth-shemesh, and that styles in fortification often change slowly, I remain unconvinced.

102. For this name see *Archaeology and the Religion of Israel*, p. 207, n. 62.

103. See Albrecht Alt, *Kleine Schriften*, III, pp. 252 ff.; Alt, "Die Staatenbildung der Israeliten in Palästina," *Kleine Schriften*, II, pp. 24 ff., 43 ff.

104. *Archaeology and the Religion of Israel*, pp. 125 ff. I have treated this subject more fully in the manuscript of my "History of the Religion of Israel" (unpublished).

105. See Samuel Klein, '*Are Hakohanim Vehalviyim, Mehqarim III, IV* (Jerusalem-Tel-Aviv, 1934) ; Albright, *Louis Ginzberg Jubilee Volume, English Section*, pp. 49 ff. See also B. Mazar, *Vetus Test. Suppl.*, VII (1960), pp. 193-205. Y. Kaufmann's view that the list of Levitic cities is utopian, going back to the times of settlement in Palestine, taken up by M. Haran (*Jour. Bib. Lit.*, LXXX [1961], pp. 45 ff., 156 ff.), does not reckon with archaeological facts or historical probability. I disagree with his view that the line adopted by P is "fictional and unreal." That it is schematic and does not always describe conditions in the time of the Tabernacle, before the building of the First Temple, I concede.

106. Cf. Albright, *ibid.*, p. 59, n. 24.

107. See *ibid.*, p. 54, with references. The fullest recent study is Max Loehr's *Das Asylwesen im Alten Testament* (1930). There can, of course, be no reasonable doubt that the individual cities of refuge were employed as asylums long before the time of David; I am here speaking of the institution of six cities, not of the origin of the practice, which was doubtless very ancient.

108. See *Archaeology and the Religion of Israel*, pp. 130 f. In Syria proper David's empire extended only to the border of Hamath in the region of Homs, but since he controlled Zobah there was no power to block him politically until he reached the Euphrates Valley. The Arameans were still partly nomadic at that time.

109. See *Archaeology and the Religion of Israel*, pp. 108, 120, with references.

110. For the chronology of this period see my treatment in *Bull. Am. Sch. Or. Res.*, No. 100, pp. 16-23. My dates are approximate, but they seem more satisfactory than any other system, precisely in part because of their flexibility, which stands in sharp contrast to the involved and rigid system of Max Vogelstein (*Biblical Chronology*, Part I, 1944). E. R. Thiele, *The Mysterious Numbers of the Hebrew Kings* (1951), is very useful, but overharmonizes in an effort to save all the numbers of the book of Kings. His system is sometimes in striking disagreement with the data of II Chron. and cannot be squared with the Tyrian chronology of Menander preserved by Josephus. On the Tyrian chronology see my discussion, *Mélanges Isidore Lévy, Annuaire de l'Institut de Philologie et d'Histoire Orientales et Slaves*, XIII (1955), pp. 1 ff.

111. For Assyrian dates see Arno Poebel, *Jour. Near East. Stud.*, 1943, p. 88. This date is further supported by O. R. Gurney, *Anat. St.*, 3 (1953), 17.

112. On the character of the Sidonian state see my discussion, *The Bible and the Ancient Near East*, pp. 341 f.

113. See *Bull. Am. Sch. Or. Res.*, No. 83, pp. 14-22, and No. 95, p. 38.

114. A bark loaded with copper ingots was recently discovered off the southwestern coast of Anatolia, and excavated by George F. Bass; see *Amer. Jour. Arch.*, 65 (1961), pp. 267 ff.

115. See Nelson Glueck, *The Other Side of the Jordan*, pp. 89-113, and for the copper mines and smelting in general see *ibid.*, pp. 50-88, and *Bull. Am. Sch. Or. Res.*, No. 90, pp. 13 f. Since then a great deal of further work has been done by Glueck, Beno Rothenberg and specialists in metallurgy, but no clear picture has yet emerged.

116. See *Archaeology of Palestine*, pp. 123 ff.; G. E. Wright, *Biblical Archaeology*, pp. 130 ff.

117. See I. Mendelsohn, *Bull. Am. Sch. Or. Res.*, No. 85, pp. 14 ff.

118. This estimate is based on the following considerations. Archaeological and documentary evidence coincides in fixing the population of Judah (as a state, not merely a tribe) in 701 B.C. at about 250,000. The Assyrian records (whose errors probably cancel out pretty well) count a little over 200,000 people in forty-six captured fortified towns of Judah (a number of towns which agrees very well both with archaeological surveys and with the total of sixty towns of significance listed in Joshua 15, which applies in my opinion to the ninth century; see now F. M. Cross, Jr., and G. E. Wright, *Jour. Bib. Lit.*, 1956, pp. 202 ff.). Tell Beit Mirsim, which represents a fair cross-section of the towns of Judah, had a maximum population in the eighth century of about 3,000 (*Tell Beit Mirsim*, III, p. 39). The total population of the captured towns may, accordingly, have been about 150,000. Allowing for a seminomadic population of about 50,000 in the Negeb and the hill-country, as well as for about the same number in Jerusalem and its surrounding villages, we should have a total of about 250,000. This agrees very well with the Assyrian total of 200,000, which did not include the people of Jerusalem or the seminomads of the Negeb, or, for that matter, the dead and the fugitives who fled into the hills. Now archaeological evidence makes it certain that there was a very considerable expansion of the population of Judah during and after the tenth century B.C., when the *pax Davidica* made it possible to found many new towns and villages. Moreover, the tremendous commercial and industrial expansion under Solomon also brought about an increase of population. Furthermore, as J. L. Kelso points out to me, the introduction of the iron plow tip, replacing tips of holm oak and copper, made it possible to increase the production of the soil very materially at that time (much as happened in Western Europe after the Dark Ages, when the introduction of the large plowshare and colter revolutionized agriculture). I have suggested elsewhere (*Jour. Pal. Or. Soc.*, 1925, pp. 20-25) that the two census reports of Numbers may reflect divergent recensions of the Davidic census, which in that case totaled about 600,000 Israelites, distributed among the twelve tribes. Some 125,000 of these are credited to the territory included

by Josh. 15 in Judah (that is, the state, not the tribe in the narrow sense). If this is right, we are warranted in deducing that the population of the southern tribes had roughly doubled between about 975 and 701 B.C., especially since this deduction agrees strikingly with archaeological indications. An increase of a fourth to a third seems conservative for the generation following the Davidic census, so we may estimate that the entire native Israelite population in the middle of Solomon's reign was at least three-quarters of a million. For a different interpretation of the census lists, see G. E. Mendenhall, *Jour. Bib. Lit.*, 77 (1958), pp. 52 ff.

119. On this subject see Alt, "Staatenbildung," *Kleine Schriften*, II, p. 44, n. 4, with the references, and my discussion, *Archaeology and the Religion of Israel*, pp. 140 ff.

120. For Babylonian parallels to Solomon's provisioning system see R. P. Dougherty, *Annual Am. Sch. Or. Res.*, V, pp. 23 ff.

121. J, E, JE, D, P are symbols used by Biblical scholars in referring to different documents incorporated in the Pentateuch. The designations are purely descriptive.

122. See my treatment of this text, *Bull. Am. Sch. Or. Res.*, No. 92, pp. 16-26; *ANET*, p. 320.

123. For the chronology see above, n. 110.

124. See *Bull. Am. Sch. Or. Res.*, No. 49, pp. 26 ff.

125. For this date see *Bull. Am. Sch. Or. Res.*, No. 130, pp. 4 ff., No. 141, pp. 26 f.

126. See Beyer, *Zeits. Deutsch. Paläst. Ver.*, 1931, pp. 113-134.

127. Cf. *Tell Beit Mirsim*, III, p. 38, n. 14, and the literature there cited. On the Shishak list see especially B. Mazar, *Vetus Test. Suppl.*, IV (1956), pp. 57 ff.

128. Cf. *Jour. Pal. Or. Soc.*, 1925, pp. 37-44.

129. On the same principle that David chose Jerusalem, which lay outside the native Israelite tribal system, as his capital, in order to free himself from tribal jealousy and intrigue as much as possible; see above, n. 103.

130. See *From the Stone Age to Christianity*, 1957 ed., pp. 298 ff.

131. On the cherubim see the literature cited in *Archaeology and the Religion of Israel*, p. 216, n. 65.

132. Cf. *Archaeology and the Religion of Israel*, pp. 157 ff. On the relationship between the queen mother, Maachah, and Kings Abijah and Asa see S. Yeivin, *Bull. Jew. Pal. Explor. Soc.*, 1943, pp. 116 ff.

133. In the light of the steadily increasing evidence for the historicity of most of the documentary material not found in Kings which is preserved by the Chronicler, it is hypercritical to reject the clear statements of II Chron. 19:8-11. See my remarks in the *Alexander Marx Jubilee Volume* (1950), pp. 61 ff.

134. See J. W. Crowfoot, Kathleen Kenyon and E. L. Sukenik, *The Buildings at Samaria* (1942), pp. 5 ff. See also G. E. Wright, *Bull. Am. Sch. Or. Res.*, No. 155, pp. 13 ff., who discusses K. Kenyon's

views in J. W. Crowfoot, G. M. Crowfoot and K. Kenyon, *The Objects from Samaria* (1957), pp. 94 ff., 198 ff.

135. For efforts to reconstruct the historical sequence of events and their causes cf. Julian Morgenstern, *Amos Studies*, I, pp. 258-348, and Alfred Jepsen, *Archiv f. Orientf.*, XIV (1942), 153-172.

136. See Levi della Vida and the writer, *Bull. Am. Sch. Or. Res.*, No. 90, pp. 30 ff. On the cult of Baal-Melcarth see the illuminating observations of R. de Vaux, *Bulletin du Musée de Beyrouth*, V, 7-20. For the text, see also *ANET*, 2nd ed., p. 501.

137. Cf. *Bull. Am. Sch. Or. Res.*, No. 94, p. 30 and n. 4. There are many additional passages in Keret II and Danel (Aqhat) where the appellation *Qudshu* (*Qodesh*), "Holiness," appears as the name of Asherah.

138. A different view is taken by Poebel, *Jour. Near East. Stud.*, 1943, pp. 80-84, but I cannot agree with his argument.

139. *Amos Studies*, pp. 161 ff.

140. See *Bull. Am. Sch. Or. Res.*, No. 44, pp. 8-10, with the references there.

141. See Nelson Glueck, *Bull. Am. Sch. Or. Res.*, No. 72, pp. 7 ff.; No. 79, pp. 13 ff., with my remarks in n. 9. See also N. Avigad, *ibid.*, No. 163, pp. 18 ff.

142. See my discussion, *Bull. Am. Sch. Or. Res.*, No. 100 (1945), p. 18, n. 8, as well as B. Landsberger, *Sam'al* (1948), p. 22, n. 42, and J. Bright, *History of Israel*, pp. 252 f. See most recently the valuable article by H. Tadmor, *Scripta Hierosolymitana*, VIII (1961), pp. 232-271. The divergencies between us are mainly the result of chronological differences.

143. Cf. *Bull. Am. Sch. Or. Res.*, No. 140, pp. 34 f.

144. According to R. Borger, *Jour. Near East. Stud.*, 19 (1960), pp. 49-53, the cuneiform writing of the name should be read Re'e rather than Sib'e. He makes a strong case, but serious difficulties remain.

145. It cannot be emphasized too strongly that the expression "Jehu son of Omri" in Assyrian means simply "Jehu of Beth-Omri," and has nothing to do with the man Omri as such: cf. *Jour. Pal. Or. Soc.*, 1921, p. 55, n. 1, where I first pointed out this obvious fact; see also *ibid.*, 1925, p. 37. The principle was discovered in Assyrian and Aramaic texts by A. Ungnad, *Orientalistische Literaturzeitung*, 9, pp. 224-226.

146. Cf. *Bull. Am. Sch. Or. Res.*, No. 149, pp. 33 ff.

147. This information comes from Rev. J. A. Fitzmyer, who has worked over the fragments of Tobit from Cave IV and who is a leading specialist in Imperial Aramaic.

148. The evidence for this view will be presented in a volume now in preparation.

149. See *Tell Beit Mirsim*, III, pp. 55-62.

150. Cf. I. Mendelsohn, *Bull. Am. Sch. Or. Res.*, No. 80, pp. 17-21.

151. Cf. *Bull. Am. Sch. Or. Res.*, No. 100, p. 21. This date, which seems to me the only one that can be squared with our direct biblical documentation, is also held by Mowinckel and Thiele.

152. On the chronology of the Ethiopian period see *Bull. Am. Sch. Or. Res.*, No. 130, pp. 8-11; No. 141, pp. 23-26. The most important new evidence comes from Laming Macadam's publication of the Kawa monuments of Taharqo, supplemented by publication of a statue of Shabako from the fifteenth year of his reign, and the identification of *Shilkanni* (pronounced *Silkan*) with the Egyptianizing *Osorkon* (Osorkon IV). These data fix the enthronement of Shabako in 710-709. The accession of Bocchoris then took place *c.* 715 and the invasion of Lower Egypt by the Ethiopian Piankhi is to be dated *c.* 716-715.

153. The problem of Sennacherib's campaigns against Hezekiah is still being debated; for convenient orientation see Leo Honor, *Sennacherib's Invasion of Palestine* (1926). German scholarship supports the one-campaign theory; cf. W. Rudolph, *Palästinajahrbuch*, 1929, pp. 59 ff., A. Alt, *Kleine Schriften*, II, pp. 242 ff. The latest and best defense of Winckler's two-campaign theory, to which I adhere, is given by J. Bright, *History of Israel*, pp. 282 ff.

154. It has recently been supposed that the original of these two poems was composed about the eleventh century B.C. It is true that there are archaic reminiscences, but the style is entirely different from that of Hebrew poems of the thirteenth-eleventh centuries B.C., and can scarcely be earlier than the eighth century. A date in the seventh century remains most plausible.

155. For the chronology of this period see especially C. J. Gadd, *Anat. Stud.*, VIII (1958), pp. 69 ff., and R. Borger, *Wiener Zeitschrift für die Kunde des Morgenlandes*, 55 (1959), pp. 62-76. It is now certain that Asshurbanapal died in the year 627/6 (Babylonian). Borger identifies Sin-shar-ishkun with Asshur-etel-ilani, but this seems impossible to me. The data, well marshaled by Borger, indicate that Sin-shar-ishkun considered 629, two years before his father's death, as the beginning of his reign; he may have been associated with his father as crown prince at that time. At all events, before or after his father's death, general Sin-shum-lishir headed a rebellion and placed Asshur-etel-ilani on the throne. Three years or so later, Sin-shar-ishkun succeeded his brother as king, presumably after a counter-revolt.

156. See M. Noth, *History of Israel*, pp. 271 ff. In my opinion A. Alt (*Zeit. für die alttestamentliche Wiss.*, 1927, pp. 59-81) has gone too far in referring the lists of towns in Galilee (Josh. 19) to the reign of Josiah; a number of them were destroyed in the eighth century and not reoccupied.

157. Cf. *Jour. Bib. Lit.*, 1939, pp. 184 f. H. L. Ginsberg, *Alexander Marx Jubilee Volume*, pp. 349 f., n. 12, emended both names, lo-

cating them in southern Judah. But his arguments against my view are tenuous. For example, Assyrian Aruma is nothing more or less than the pre-exilic Galilean pronunciation *Ha-rumah* for Hebrew *Ha-ramah*, "The Height."

158. On the historical situation (with references to the literature) see *Jour. Bib. Lit.*, 1932, pp. 84 ff. My treatment has not been affected here by more recent finds.

159. See now D. J. Wiseman, *Chronicles of Chaldaean Kings (626-556 B.C.)*, and my discussion, *Bull. Am. Sch. Or. Res.*, No. 143, pp. 22 ff.

160. On the historical situation see J. Bright, *Bib. Arch.*, XII (1949), pp. 46-52.

161. See Jerome D. Quinn, *Bull. Am. Sch. Or. Res.*, No. 164, pp. 19 f.

162. It must be remembered that the Chaldeans were originally East-Arabian nomads and that they employed the Proto-Arabian script as late as the sixth century B.C. in Babylonia. The Chaldean Nebuchadnezzar and Nabonidus, both of whom campaigned in Arabia, were presumably interested not only in trade routes but also in conquering the old Arabian rivals of the Chaldeans.

163. Cf. *Jour. Bib. Lit.*, 1932, pp. 90 ff.

164. See now the epochal treatment of the work of the Deuteronomist by Martin Noth, *Überlieferungsgeschichtliche Studien* (1943), pp. 3-110. The superfluous assumption, that there was a whole Deuteronomic school which collaborated over a long period, may now be discarded. However, I cannot accept Noth's date for the composition of this work about the middle of the sixth century (p. 91), since it is highly improbable that so much older historical material had survived the catastrophe of the Exile (note how little was available a century and a half later to the Chronicler!).

165. Cf. *From the Stone Age to Christianity*, 1957 ed., pp. 315 ff.

166. See my remarks in A. O. Lovejoy *et al.*, eds., *A Documentary History of Primitivism and Related Ideas*, I (1935), pp. 421-432.

167. There may be another reason for Jeremiah's support of the Babylonians. It has recently been shown by R. Labat (*Journal asiatique*, 1961, pp. 1-12) that the statement of Herodotus (i:103-106), according to which the Scythian domination of Asia for twenty-eight years came after the accession of Cyaxares, is supported by a neglected papyrus fragment from Oxyrhynchus. Since the Assyrian inscriptions of Asshurbanapal, which carry us down to *c.* 630 B.C., nowhere mention the Scythian irruption into Syria and Palestine, so vividly described by Herodotus (i:105), it is likely to have taken place during the troubled period after 625 B.C., while Jeremiah was still young. We may well suppose that the Scythian invasion left an ineffaceable impression of barbarian atrocities, beside which the oppressive Babylonian rule may have seemed beneficent. Furthermore, the Babylonian Empire stood

squarely between the Scythians of Asia Minor and Armenia, on the one hand, and Palestine, on the other. (Cf. Jer. 6:22 ff., and other passages mentioning the invasion from the north, which may now again be identified with the Scythian menace, at least in part.)

168. See *Bull. Am. Sch. Or. Res.*, No. 82, p. 22; *ANET*, pp. 321 f.

169. *Jour. Bib. Lit.*, 1932, pp. 78 f.; *Tell Beit Mirsim*, III, 65 f.; *Pal. Explor. Fund Quart. State. (Pal. Explor. Quart.)*, 1937, pp. 175 ff., 235 ff.; *ibid.*, 1938, pp. 252 ff. See also Wright, *Bib. Archaeology*, pp. 175 f.

170. See above, n. 118.

171. For this date see *Bull. Am. Sch. Or. Res.*, No. 100, p. 22; Thiele, *ibid.*, No. 143, pp. 22 ff., and the writer, *ibid.*, No. 143, pp. 31 f.

172. See Roland de Vaux, *Ancient Israel* (1961), pp. 129 ff.

173. Cf. *Bib. Arch.*, V (1942), pp. 49 ff.; *ANET*, p. 308.

174. See *Jour. Bib. Lit.*, LI (1932), pp. 100 f.; C. G. Howie, *The Date and Composition of Ezekiel* (1950), pp. 5-26.

175. See Alt, *Kleine Schriften*, II, pp. 316-337.

176. See above, n. 173, for references.

177. For this interpretation, following the Greek text, of the unintelligible "Sheshbazzar" see my observations, *Jour. Bib. Lit.*, XL (1921), pp. 108 ff., and for the initial *shin*, due to dissimilation (for which there are two other illustrations in this very name), see *Bull. Am. Sch. Or. Res.*, No. 82, p. 17.

178. Cf. particularly R. de Vaux, *Revue Biblique*, 1937, pp. 29-57, following in the wake of Eduard Meyer and H. H. Schaeder; and E. J. Bickerman, *Jour. Bib. Lit.*, LXV (1946), pp. 249 ff.

179. See Ebeling, *Aus dem Leben der jüdischen Exulanten* (1914), and Eissfeldt, *Zeits. Alttest. Wiss.*, 1935, pp. 60 f., for the material from the Murashu archives. There is a little scattered material from earlier periods, but some of it is doubtful.

180. This rough estimate is based on the following facts: Archaeological explorations have demonstrated that there was a virtually complete break in the urban life of Judah after the Chaldean invasions and deportations which ended in 582 B.C. (*e.g.*, at Debir, Lachish, Beth-shemesh, Beth-zur, Ramat Rahel, as well as at many other sites which have been explored more superficially). Even Bethel, which was outside of the pre-exilic state (except under Josiah) but inside the later Persian province, was destroyed before 522 B.C., though it was a flourishing town until the middle or late sixth century (see provisionally *Bull. Am. Sch. Or. Res.*, No. 56, p. 14; subsequent work on the pottery has shown that we are dealing with a phase which followed the Exile but preceded the developed Persian types of the fifth century). It has long been certain from careful study of the names, etc., that the list in Ezra 2 and Neh. 7 belongs to a relatively late date in the fifth century, in strict accord with Neh. 7:5 ff., which attributes the publication of the

document to Nehemiah, *c.* 440 B.C. It is, accordingly, clear that this document represents the revised form of the census of Judah, begun at the Restoration; it includes both the returned exiles (and their descendants) and the Jews already established in the district. Since the entire population, including slaves, was reckoned at just under 50,000 in *c.* 440, it was probably not over two-fifths this number three generations earlier, before natural increase and continuing influx of immigrants from the *golah* had brought it up to the higher level.

181. On the political situation at this time see Olmstead, *Am. Jour. Sem. Lang.*, 1938, pp. 409 ff., but note that his reconstruction was totally recast in his *History of the Persian Empire* (1948), pp. 135-143. In the light of our increased knowledge of tablet dates, conveniently summarized by R. A. Parker and W. H. Dubberstein in their latest survey, *Babylonian Chronology: 626 B.C.–A.D. 75* (1956), pp. 15 f., it may well be, however, that we must raise the dates in Haggai by a year, assuming that Jerusalem then dated by the accession year of Darius instead of his enthronement year. In this case, there would be close synchronism between the rebellion of Nebuchadnezzar IV (August, 521–late November, 521) and the prophecies of Haggai (late August–end of December, 521), if we suppose that Haggai 2:20 ff. (not dated to a given month) actually dates to the sixth or seventh instead of the ninth month; see Haggai 1:15; 2:1.

182. The native name of Sardis was *Sfarda*, written in the Lydian-Aramaic bilingual of Sardis exactly as in Obad. 20. The Aramaic inscription in question dates probably from the year 455 (C. C. Torrey, *Am. Jour. Sem. Lang.*, XXXIV, pp. 191 ff.) and may reflect a Jewish-Aramaic community settled there (Kahle and Sommer, *Kleinasiatische Forschungen*, I, 29 f.). There can be little doubt, in my opinion, that the prophecy of Obadiah reflects the end of the sixth or the beginning of the fifth century B.C.

183. See John Bright, *A History of Israel*, pp. 375-386, and *Yehezkel Kaufmann Jubilee Volume* (1960), pp. 70-87.

184. Cf. R. Kittel, *Geschichte des Volkes Israel*, III, pt. 2, pp. 614 f.

185. Thanks to the work of Howorth, Torrey and especially of Sigmund Mowinckel, *Stattholderen Nehemia* (Kristiania, 1916), it has become almost certain that the biblical text followed by Josephus in his account of the Restoration was the original Alexandrian translation of the second century B.C., the first part of which is preserved in First Esdras (Third Esdras in the Latin Bible). The extant Greek text of Nehemiah goes back only to Theodotion in the second century A.D. Torrey and others have already seen that First Esdras preserves many details which have been lost or corrupted in the Hebrew recension of Ezra (which is better in other ways). Mowinckel is, therefore, quite justified (pp. 58 ff.) in pre-

ferring Josephus's chronological data to those of the Hebrew Bible; see below, n. 186.

186. According to the Hebrew the wall was begun fifty-two days before the twenty-fifth of Elul, *i.e.*, about the third of Ab, the fifth month. According to Josephus (Ant. xi, §179, Loeb ed.) it was finished after two years and four months, in the ninth month, which would mean that it was begun in the fifth month.

187. See above, n. 175.

188. On the history of the house of Tobiah, illuminated in recent decades by the systematic study of the remains at 'Araq el-Emir and by the Zeno Papyri, see especially the work of Vincent, Gressmann and Koenig referred to in my *Archaeology of Palestine and the Bible*, pp. 221 f., nn. 108-111. See further my *Archaeology of Palestine*, p. 149 (the dates there given are confirmed by F. M. Cross, Jr., *The Bible and the Ancient Near East*, p. 195, n. 75, and supported by Paul Lapp, *Bull. Am. Sch. Or. Res.*, No. 165, pp. 33 f.).

189. On the religion of the Jewish colony at Elephantine see most recently Albert Vincent, *La religion des Judéo-Araméens d'Éléphantine* (1937), and my observations in *Archaeology and the Religion of Israel*, pp. 168-174, as well as *Bull. Am. Sch. Or. Res.*, No. 90, p. 40 (where I take account of the new data provided by the article of U. Cassuto in *Kedem*, I, 47-52). The close cultic sympathy existing between the Jews of Elephantine and the people of Samaria is illustrated not only by the way in which the former appeal to the latter after the destruction of their temple, but also by numerous more general considerations, on which cf. also Van Hoonacker, *Une communauté judéo-Araméenne à Éléphantine* (1915), pp. 73-84. On the whole subject see most recently the comprehensive survey by E. G. Kraeling, *The Brooklyn Museum Aramaic Papyri* (1953), pp. 83-99.

190. See especially H. L. Allrik, *Bull. Am. Sch. Or. Res.*, No. 136, pp. 21 ff.

191. The "governor of Moab" after whom the family in question had received its name must have flourished under the Babylonian or the Persian Empire, since the word *pehah* was borrowed by the Arameans in Late Assyrian times, whereas Moab was still ruled by its own tributary kings down at least to *c*. 645 B.C.

192. The official publication of this excavation will be issued soon.

193. Assuming that "seventh year" (Ezra 7:7) is haplography of "thirty-seventh year" (note that the latter would have three initial occurrences of *shin* following one another, as in Neh. 5:14). My earlier view that Ezra's mission took place in the seventh year of Artaxerxes II, in which I followed Van Hoonacker (*Jour. Bib. Lit.*, XL [1921], pp. 104-124), has since been replaced by a position approximating that of Bertholet (*The Archaeology of Palestine and the Bible* [1932], pp. 169 ff., 218 f., n. 98), though I have

not always adhered consistently to this position. There is no adequate reason to follow Torrey and delete the reference to Nehemiah as *tirshatha* in Neh. 8:9, which deals with Ezra's reform, or to separate Neh. 10:1 from it. It follows that Nehemiah was then in Jerusalem, whether before the expiration of his twelve-year period or not. Mowinckel thought (on the basis of the chronology preserved by Josephus; see above, n. 125) that Nehemiah's twelve years as governor may have expired in the thirty-seventh year, assuming that he took office in the twenty-fifth year, but this alternative is uncertain. In any event, it seems highly probable that Ezra arrived in Jerusalem toward the end of Nehemiah's governorship. With this date would, incidentally, harmonize very well the fact that he was accompanied by the Davidide Hattush, son of Shechaniah, who was probably born between 490 and 480 B.C. and would thus be between fifty and sixty at this time. With it would also agree very well the reference (Ezra 10:6) to the "chamber of Johanan son of Eliashib," who was High Priest when the first edition of the work of the Chronicler was finished (Neh. 12:23), since Eliashib was still High Priest at the return of Nehemiah to the court in 432 (Neh. 13:4 ff.), whereas Johanan had apparently been High Priest for some time in 411 B.C., to judge from the Elephantine correspondence. [This remains the same as printed in 1949, but there have been some very important treatments by John Bright, referred to in n. 183 above.]

194. See the preceding note. The Ezra Memoirs proper are couched in the first person, whereas the references to Ezra in connection with Nehemiah are in the third person.

195. Cf. Eduard Meyer, *Die Entstehung des Judentums*; *Der Papyrusfund von Elephantine*; H. H. Schaeder, *Esra der Schreiber*.

196. Cf. Albert Vincent, *La Religion des Judéo-Araméens d'Éléphantine*, pp. 235 ff.

197. See Torrey, *Composition and Historical Value of Ezra-Nehemiah*, pp. 16-28, etc., *Ezra Studies*, pp. 238-248; Albright, *Jour. Bib. Lit.*, 1921, pp. 119 f.; Arvid Kapelrud, *The Question of Authorship in the Ezra Narrative* (Oslo, 1944), pp. 95 ff. The last-mentioned scholar tries to avoid the conclusion which Torrey reached by severe logic, that the Ezra Memoirs are apocryphal (whereas I believe that Ezra was the Chronicler), by speaking of "Chronicler circles." Just what "circles" of scholars we can expect in a largely agricultural community of considerably less than a hundred thousand souls is not clear. Martin Noth emphasizes the individuality of the Chronicler very strongly in his *Überlieferungsgeschichtliche Studien* (1943), pp. 155 ff.

198. Cf. already *Jour. Bib. Lit.*, XL (1921), p. 111. Pushing back the birth of Pedaiah to before 592 B.C., as required by the new cuneiform evidence, and allowing (in view of the fact that not all members of the genealogical chain in I Chron. 3:17 ff. were first-

born sons) between twenty-five and thirty (*i.e.*, twenty-seven and a half) years to a generation (plus a decade for the younger sons of Elioenai), we come to about 420 for the birth of the youngest son of Elioenai in our list.

199. Cf. *The Archaeology of Palestine and the Bible*, pp. 173 ff.; *Bull. Am. Sch. Or. Res.*, No. 53, pp. 20 ff.; *Jour. Bib. Lit.*, LXI (1942), pp. 125 f.; J. Kutsher, *Kedem*, II, p. 74. In the leather scrolls published by G. R. Driver (*Aramaic Documents of the Fifth Century* B.C., [1954], p. 17), the word *pitgama* or *patgama* (which Torrey and Cowley, followed by many others, regarded as decisive evidence for the Greek date of the Chronicler, since they erroneously identified it with different Greek words) appears twice in a Persian phrase which means approximately "bad matter."

200. On these coins see M. Narkiss, *Matbeat Hayehudim* (Jerusalem, 1936), Book I, pp. 17-23. Besides the coins, we have a rapidly increasing number of pottery stamps with the inscription *Yehud*, "Judah," some of which clearly belong to the fourth century B.C., while others may come from the third century. On these seal impressions and the fourth-century seals of the governor of Judah (who seems to have been Jewish at that time), see my discussion, *Bull. Am. Sch. Or. Res.*, No. 148, pp. 28 ff., and especially Y. Aharoni, *Excavations at Ramat Rahel* (Rome, 1962), pp. 56-59.

201. Cf. *From the Stone Age to Christianity*, 1957 ed., pp. 337 f. Cf. also E. J. Bickerman, in *The Jews; Their History, Culture and Religion* (1949), p. 87.

Chronological Table of the Divided Monarchy

Judah

Rehoboam	8[17]	c. 922-915
Abijah (Abijam)	3	c. 915-913
Asa	41	c. 913-873
Jehoshaphat	25	c. 873-849
Jehoram	8	c. 849-842
Ahaziah	1	c. *842*
Athaliah	6[7]	c. *842*-837
Jehoash	38[40]	c. 837-800
Amaziah	18[29]	c. 800-783
Uzziah (Azariah)	42[52]	c. 783-742
Jotham (regent)	8 (?)	c. 750-742
Jotham (king)	8—[16]	c. 742-735
Jehoahaz I (Ahaz)	21±[16]	c. 735-*715*
Hezekiah	29	c. *715*-687

(Here begins post-dating in Judah)

Manasseh	45[55]	c. 687-642
Amon	2	c. 642-640
Josiah	31	č. 640-*609*
Jehoahaz II (Shallum)	3 mos.	*609*
Jehoiakim (Eliakim)	11	*609-598*
Jehoiachin (Jeconiah)	3 mos.	598-597 [Julian]
Zedekiah (Mattaniah)	11	598/7-587/6 [Babylonian]

Israel

Jeroboam I	22	c. 922-901
Nadab	2	c. 901-900
Baasha	24	c. 900-877
Elah	2	c. 877-876
Zimri	7 days	c. 876
Omri	8[12]	c. 876-869
Ahab	20[22]	c. 869-850
Ahaziah	2	c. 850-849
Joram	8[12]	c. 849-*842*
Jehu	28	c. *842*-815
Joahaz	15[17]	c. 815-801
Joash	16	c. 801-786
Jeroboam II	41	c. 786-746
Zechariah	6 mos.	c. 746-745
Shallum	1 mo.	c. 745
Menahem	10	c. 745-*736*
Pekahiah	2	c. *736-735*
Pekah	4 (?) [20]	c. *735-732*
Hoshea	9	c. *732-724*
Fall of Samaria		*722/1*

The above is from "The Chronology of the Divided Monarchy of Israel" by W. F. Albright *and first appeared in the* BULLETIN OF THE AMERICAN SCHOOLS OF ORIENTAL RESEARCH, No. 100, December 1945, *pages 16 through 22. Individual dates have been revised to agree with subsequent discoveries. Unrecorded coregencies are possible in some cases, but do not affect the over-all chronology. Italicized dates are certain within a year or so.*

INDEX